70TH ANNIVERSARY EDITION

IMAGES
of America
THE LAKE MICHIGAN
CAR FERRY *BADGER*

T0273958

Having just arrived at Kewaunee's south ferry slip, the *Badger* takes a break from her sea trials on March 16, 1953. She took on her first load of coal cars to fuel her bunkers and later posed for publicity photos on Lake Michigan with her twin, the *Spartan*. (Courtesy John W. Hausmann Collection.)

70TH ANNIVERSARY EDITION

IMAGES
of America

THE LAKE MICHIGAN CAR FERRY *BADGER*

Arthur Chavez

ARCADIA
PUBLISHING

Published by Arcadia Publishing
Charleston, South Carolina

Printed in the United States of America

Library of Congress Catalog Card Number: 2023933572

For all general information contact Arcadia Publishing at:
Telephone 843-853-2070
Fax 843-853-0044
E-mail sales@arcadiapublishing.com
For customer service and orders:
Toll-Free 1-888-313-2665

Visit us on the Internet at www.arcadiapublishing.com

In memory of Capt. Bernard A. Robertson
(1906–1992)

Capt. Bernard A. "Bunny" Robertson enjoys the company of this group of models on the bridge of the *Badger*, c. 1960. This was a part of the Chesapeake & Ohio Railway's print and motion picture media campaign promoting its cross-lake car ferry operations. "The Golden Link," a 16-mm film designed to attract freight shippers, was created during these photo shoots. (Courtesy Capt. Bernard Robertson Collection.)

CONTENTS

ACKNOWLEDGMENTS

I've learned a great deal about car ferries from Audrey (Robertson) Boals, Pat Brandon, John Brandt, Terry Bruce, Andrew Buelow, James Cabot, Bill Christopher, Dan Cramer, Steve and Carol Elve, Jim Fay, Tim Foster, Roger Genson, Jim Gregorski, Bruce Groeneveld, Jed Jaworski, Steve Johnson, Max and JoLynn Hanley, Bill Hansen, Heidi Hansen, John Hausmann, Frank Heine, George Hilton, Dan Hoenecke, Joan Kloster, Michael Leon, Dan Luedke, Stephen McMillan, Mike Modderman, Jim Nelson, Stephanie Parkinson, Dave Petersen, John P. Praedel, Tom Read, Floyd Schmidt, Fred Schmitt, Tom Schuller, Linda Spencer, Trevor Suarez, Bob Strauss, Rich Swagel, John Teichmoeller, Jerry Tyler, Bob Vande Vusse, Marc and Jill Vander Meulen, Roxy Weinand, Chris Winters, and Tom and Sue Younk.

I was kindly granted access to these research facilities by June Larsen and Kay Dragan at the Door County Maritime Museum; Suzette Lopez at the Milwaukee Public Library; Cathy Green, Kevin Cullen, and Hannah Patten at the Wisconsin Maritime Museum; and Steve Begnoche, David Bossick, Patti Klevorn, Paul Peterson and Todd Reed of the *Ludington Daily News*. Permission to reproduce images was given by Nicholas Blenkey, editor, *Marine/Log*; Sam Steiner, engineering manager, Skinner Engine Company; and Steve Lavin, vice president/general manager, WBAY in Green Bay.

Jim Anderson, Terri Brown, Don Clingan, Charles Conrad, Lynda Daugherty-Matson, Judy Evans, Thom Hawley, Kari Karr, Bob Manglitz, Sharla Manglitz, and Jean McCumber of Lake Michigan Carferry were beyond helpful through my years of knowing them. I also owe a debt of gratitude to Sara Spore, Mark Barker and Chrissy Kadleck of Interlake Maritime Services. Huge thanks to Shelby Soberalski, director of marketing and sales at LMC, for her enthusiastic support and interest in this project. Among the *Badger*'s crew, past and present, who shared with me their thoughts, are Mike Braybrook, Everett Dust, Bruce Eddy, Marylin Greiner, Danny Hecko, Jake Huggard, Dave Lilleberg, Colleen McCauley, Ted Schultz, Ray Short, Don Short, Bob Weinert, Captains Gregg Andersen, Ernest Barth, John Bissell, Jeff Curtis, Jim Hinds, Dean Hobbs, Michael Martin, Bruce Masse, Bernard Robertson, Walter Skibin, and Warren Stowe. The chief engineers are Charles Cart, Kevin Diedrich, Theron Haas, Bill Kulka, John Leindecker, and Jim Luke. These fine people have expanded my car ferry knowledge. My sincere apologies to those I haven't the space here to include but who are named in my other books. To all, you have my profound gratitude.

I appreciate Maura Brown, my first editor at Arcadia Publishing 20 years ago. She believed in car ferries from the beginning, after my brief but apparently convincing presentation at Arcadia's former Chicago regional office. Months later, upon submission of the completed manuscript, photos, and layout planner, Maura turned to me and wondered aloud if people would still be interested in and reading my book "20 years from now?" Jeff Ruetsche did the heavy lifting to pitch this 70th anniversary edition idea to his colleagues at Arcadia. I owe a tremendous debt to IT expert and friend, Father Tim Oudenhoven. His skilled wizardry at enhancing dusty old slide transparencies and breathing into them new life is extraordinary. My car ferry history journey sails onward with lifelong friends Ken, Trish, and Kristin Ottmann, Doug Goodhue, Tony Robles, Dan Bissell, and Gregg Andersen; together we witnessed the final years of the Lake Michigan railroad car ferries and the beginning of the *Badger*'s new era. Lastly, my heartfelt love goes out to my parents Peter and Linda, my siblings, my wife Faith, and my daughter Lydia.

INTRODUCTION

The Lake Michigan car ferry *Badger* is a holdout from the lost era of large Great Lakes passenger ships. That she survives today on her 70th anniversary providing an important seasonal transportation alternative is a tribute to her owners and dedicated crewmembers. In her intended role, that of carrying loaded railroad freight cars, she is long past her prime. But in her current role carrying tourists and their autos, in addition to buses and commercial tractor/trailers, she is just hitting her stride.

The *Badger* is the last operating vessel of a once large fleet of cross-lake railroad car ferries that began modestly with a single ship, only five years after this type of craft was introduced on the Great Lakes. The Michigan-based Pere Marquette Railroad pioneered the use of modern, steel-hulled deepwater car ferries with the launching of the steamer *Pere Marquette*. Placed into service in February 1897, the coal-fired ferry began the historic 60-mile run between Ludington and Manitowoc. By the early 1900s, the fleet had grown to six vessels and had surpassed its rivals in terms of size and sophistication of operation. The PM was so successful that its marine managers were consulted by international ferry operators who sought advice on vessel construction, maintenance, dispatching, and icebreaking techniques. Representatives from Finland, Russia, Sweden, and Great Britain made periodic visits to observe the service firsthand. From that point forward, the ferry fleet headquartered at Ludington would dominate Lake Michigan's railroad-owned network of car ferries.

At various times between 1897 and 1947, the Pere Marquette operated a total of 13 ferries on Lake Michigan, running between Ludington and the Wisconsin ports of Milwaukee, Manitowoc, and Kewaunee. The routes varied between 60 and 97 miles in length and were often plagued by violent storms and heavy ice. Given the fact that most of the cross-lake runs were made at speeds of 12 to 14 miles per hour, a remarkable volume of freight was carried. In those 50 years, the Pere Marquette car ferries made over 160,000 lake crossings and transported roughly 4.5 million railroad carloads with a total of over 75 million tons of freight. These numbers represent a somewhat conservative estimate, as records from the earliest few years of service no longer exist. While freight cars were the primary reason for their existence, tourism began to play an important factor in the evolution of the car ferries. With the advent of the automobile and the development of roadways that were conducive to regional and cross-country touring, the ferries began catering to this lucrative trade in the mid 1920s. As new car ferries replaced their aging predecessors, greater emphasis was placed in passenger dining facilities and overnight sleeping accommodations. The ships soon earned a reputation for excellent cuisine complete with china, white-jacketed waiters and gold-braided, uniformed stewards, pursers, and deck officers.

In 1947, the Chesapeake & Ohio Railway absorbed its subsidiary, the Pere Marquette Railway, including its marine operations. By 1950, the C&O Railway had embarked on an ambitious fleet expansion program including the modernization of two existing ships and the construction of two new ones. The latter were the *Badger* and her twin sister *Spartan*; the last large coal-burning passenger ships built in the United States. (The *Badger* holds the distinction of being one of the last operating coal-burning passenger steamers in the world, but may soon be repowered for efficiency, fuel economy and environmental stewardship). Through the 1950s and 1960s, the *Badger* and her six fleetmates carried thousands of passengers and autos while at the same time carrying railroad cars laden with millions of tons of freight produced by industrial manufacturers, food plants, and fuel processors from throughout the United States and Canada. The new twin C&O ferries added significantly to Ludington's total passenger and tonnage figures already well established earlier by the PM fleet.

By the mid-1970s, the C&O and its rival Lake Michigan ferry operators contended that their services were no longer economical to operate. Higher operating costs in the face of more efficient all-rail routes had rendered car ferries obsolete. Service frequency was reduced and many of the older ships were retired and sold for scrap. Vocal protests by freight shippers, city and state governments, and local chambers of commerce brought a great deal of media attention to the imminent loss of the ferry service. Their opposition only delayed the inevitable. The ferry operators were ultimately successful in their abandonment efforts, with routes systematically abolished beginning in 1978. C&O's last run was slated for abandonment in the summer of 1983.

All appeared hopeless, but in July 1983 the remaining three ships in C&O's fleet were sold to a group of investors headed by Ludington hotel owner Glen F. Bowden and construction contractor George L. Towns. The new venture, the Michigan-Wisconsin Transportation Company, initially operated the *Badger* and *City of Midland 41* between Ludington and Milwaukee and Ludington and Kewaunee, respectively. Within two years, Bowden had become sole proprietor and scaled back the service to one route, Ludington to Kewaunee, served by one car ferry, alternating between the *Badger* and the *Midland*. By 1989, much of M-WT's rail freight contracts were lost to the price-competitive trucking industry, thus forcing the cessation of service

Cross-lake railroad ferry service ended on November16, 1990, when the *Badger* made the final freight crossing between Kewaunee and Ludington, thus closing the final chapter of a near century-old institution. Once again, with her status uncertain, the future looked grim for Ludington's last remaining ferry. Bowden struggled to reinstate M-WT's presence on the lake. Unsuccessful in obtaining union concessions from his crew, as well as new freight agreements with shippers, he was forced into bankruptcy.

In 1992, retired Michigan industrialist Charles Conrad stepped in to resurrect the ferry service. Instead of resuming service to Kewaunee, a route was established to Manitowoc. His new firm, Lake Michigan Carferry Service, Inc., thoroughly refurbished the *Badger's* lounge and dining facilities to cater exclusively to the tourist trade. The ship's railcar handling capacity and equipment were removed and was outfitted to carry passengers, autos, recreational vehicles, commercial trucks and motor coaches.

In the 20 years since Mr. Conrad formed LMC, much has taken place, including the ship reaching her golden anniversary in 2003. The *Badger* was rechristened by Sharla Manglitz, granddaughter of Charles, and accompanied by her mother Janet and grandmother Elsie Conrad in a festive public ceremony, followed by celebratory events throughout the city.

In 2009, the *Badger* was placed on the National Register of Historic Places, followed by the official designation in 2016 as a National Historic Landmark by the US Department of the Interior. And, in 2020, Lake Michigan Carferry Service was acquired by Interlake Maritime Services, parent firm of Interlake Steamship Company and its well-managed, highly maintained fleet of Great Lakes bulk self-unloading ships. This new ownership ensures a bright future for the *Badger*, as investments in improving and upgrading the ship have already been made, and further improvements will continue.

What follows is a pictorial chronicle of the *Badger's* life and times.

One
FLEET HISTORY
1897–1950

Annarbor Car Ferry No. 1. This boat was the first of a large fleet of car ferries that now ply the open waters on the Great Lakes

No. 33032 Moore & Gibson Co., New York — Germany

The Toledo Ann Arbor & Northern Michigan Railroad established Lake Michigan car ferry service in November 1892. Their wooden-hulled ice-reinforced steamer, *Ann Arbor No. 1* is shown at Kewaunee, Wisconsin, c. late-1890s. With a capacity for 22 loaded railcars, the No. 1 and twin sister *Ann Arbor No. 2* opened a cross-lake freight gateway between Kewaunee and Frankfort, Michigan, connecting to points east and west. (Courtesy Robert Strauss Collection.)

No. 877. Franz Huld, Publisher, New York

Winter Scene in Frankfort, Mich.

Viewed with skepticism by investors and prospective freight shippers, the concept of the open-water railroad ferry had a difficult time coming to fruition. Through his tenacity, Ann Arbor president James M. Ashley was able to secure financing for the construction of two ships from the outset, despite the vagaries of the operation. He also convinced the coal supplier for his road's locomotives to send a few cars as the *Ann Arbor No. 1's* inaugural "guinea" cargo. Until proven otherwise, scenes like this depicting the *No. 1* icebound, c. 1900, were in the minds of early, time-conscious freight shippers. (Courtesy Tom Read Collection.)

Vindicated by the success of his car ferry venture, James Ashley's dream caught the fancy of other regional railroad companies. By the early 1900s, there were cross-lake railroad ferry services on Lakes Erie and Ontario, and an exceptionally high concentration on Lake Michigan. *Ann Arbor No. 2* is shown aground on a sandbar at Frankfort, Michigan, c. 1902. *Ann Arbor No. 3* is in the background, transferring aboard some of *No. 2's* cargo. (Courtesy Arthur Ackerman Collection.)

After watching the trials of the Ann Arbor fleet, the Flint & Pere Marquette Railroad, which had previous experience running a line of bulk freighters, introduced its own car ferry in early 1897. The 350-foot *Pere Marquette* was placed on a 60-mile run between Ludington, Michigan and Manitowoc, Wisconsin. The lone ferry initially ran as a complement to the freighters, but in time it replaced them after demonstrating superior performance, both in icebreaking ability and operating efficiency. Shown is one of the Flint & Pere Marquette's first advertisements that highlighted both its car ferry and "propeller" (package freighter) lines, c. 1897. (Author's collection.)

Designed by naval architect Robert Logan and Flint & Pere Marquette's marine superintendent Capt. James W. Martin (who died of pneumonia just five weeks after the ferry's February 16, 1897 maiden voyage), the *Pere Marquette* is shown entering Manitowoc c. 1899. Her design was so successful that F&PM's successor, the Pere Marquette Railroad, built a fleet of ships based on her prototype. By 1903 the PM Railroad had five Logan-designed steel-hulled car ferries plus one wooden one inherited during its corporate restructuring. (Courtesy Wisconsin Maritime Museum at Manitowoc.)

Shown entering the wooden piers lining the channel at Ludington harbor, the *Pere Marquette* completes another crossing from Wisconsin, c. 1901. The east-west Lake Michigan ferry routes were a time-saving advantage over the land-based rail lines that invariably passed through the congested Chicago rail yards. Delays of up to two or three days were not unheard of. (Author's collection.)

The success of the Pere Marquette car ferry fleet lies in large part to the dedication and leadership of marine superintendent William L. Mercereau. He served in this capacity from 1899 until his retirement, due to failing eyesight, in 1931. Building the fleet from one car ferry and four bulk freighters to a roster of nine car ferries at the time of his departure, Mercereau was highly regarded throughout the international maritime circles as an authority on car ferry operation. He recognized the potential of his ferry crews and often lured officers away from rival Lake Michigan ferry lines. He also surrounded himself with an excellent maintenance and shore-based support staff. (Courtesy Pere Marquette Historical Society, Robert Vande Vusse Collection.)

One of the best skippers of the PM fleet was Capt. W.H. Van Dyke, shown here in a bearskin coat on the bridge wing of the *Pere Marquette 17*, c. 1921. He lost his right arm in a hunting accident, yet was not hindered in his ability to manipulate the dual-engine control telegraphs during critical docking procedures. (Courtesy Andy Perrault Collection.)

One of the hazards of year-round Great Lakes navigation was a heavy field of ice. The car ferries were heavily constructed to overcome this obstacle. They were delayed frequently, usually by a matter of hours and only on rare occasions by several days. *Pere Marquette 19* is shown mired in a field of sheet ice, c. 1911. Several crewmen are seen using pike poles to create cracks in the ice along the ship's hull. (Courtesy Art MacLaren Collection.)

Most of Robert Logan's ferries were designed with little or no passenger accommodations. *Pere Marquette 17* and *Pere Marquette 18*, shown here, were the exception, being designed with cabins for the overnight runs between Ludington and Milwaukee. With the growth of the PM fleet, more routes were established. Ludington to Milwaukee was added in 1900, Ludington to Kewaunee in 1903. The *18* is shown on an excursion run at Waukegan, Illinois, c. 1908. (Author's collection.)

During periods of low freight traffic during the summer months, the *Pere Marquette 18* was chartered for July and August excursions between 1907 and 1910. She ran day trips from her base at Chicago to Waukegan, Illinois, carrying up to 5,000 passengers. Upon the completion of the 1910 excursion season, the *18* was placed back on its usual freight run to Milwaukee. On its first trip out, the *18* mysteriously sank 20 miles offshore from Sheboygan, Wisconsin with the loss of 29 lives. (Author's collection.)

Pere Marquette 19 is shown entering Ludington harbor during the "Million Dollar Harbor Jubilee" on July 4, 1914. The public celebration was held in honor of the US government-funded improvements to the harbor. Improvements included extensive dredging and the construction of concrete breakwater arms at the harbor entrance. This helped to drastically reduce the number of groundings on sandbars by the PM car ferries. (Courtesy James Cabot Collection.)

The Pere Marquette car ferry fleet was the largest beneficiary of the harbor improvements. Consequently, the ferries were active participants during the celebration. The fleet's marine superintendent, W.L. Mercereau, was instrumental in lobbying Congress for the budget appropriations for the renovation program. His fleets' annually increasing tonnage figures justified his request. *Pere Marquette 17* is shown heading out the channel. (Courtesy James Cabot Collection.)

Railroad cars were the primary reason for the existence of the car ferries. Each ship could carry approximately 30 standard-sized (for the time) railcars. Switch engines could unload and reload a ferry in a little over an hour. *Pere Marquette 17* is shown being loaded at Ludington's south (No. 2) slip, c. 1914. (Courtesy James Cabot Collection.)

Crewmen on the car ferries were often drawn from the farms and small towns surrounding the ports they served. Early crews typically worked a watch for six hours on duty and six hours off, seven days a week. Consequently, there was a high turnover rate, especially among the lower ratings. No vacations were granted; a crewmember simply signed on and off at will. Two young crewmen enjoy a break in the action on the aft spar deck of the *Pere Marquette 17*, c. early 1920s. (Courtesy Dave Lilleberg Collection.)

Ice was not the only obstacle the car ferries faced. Heavy seas were often encountered on Lake Michigan. Waves could easily build to 20 feet in height during the fall and winter months. The ship captains seldom laid-in for weather. They simply headed out and kept their bows into the seas in an effort to maintain schedules, if a particular cargo was time-sensitive. *Pere Marquette 17* is shown plowing into a swell during a storm in October 1929. (Author's collection.)

During the 1920s, larger and faster ships gradually replaced the older car ferries in the Pere Marquette fleet. Here, the *Pere Marquette 19* lies in the lay-up slip at Ludington, c. post-1930. Scenes like this were becoming more common, particularly during the Great Depression. (Author's collection.)

The Railroad on Lake Michigan

Trans Michigan Route.

Pere Marquette System.

Seven of These Staunch Car Ferries Ply the Year Round

MILWAUKEE, Manitowoc and Kewaunee on the Wisconsin side of Lake Michigan, and Ludington on the Michigan shore, form the terminals on that body of water for three main lines of the Pere Marquette Railway, which is a rather unique system of transportation, since the fleet of car ferries transfers the cars over these long distances. This idea, which was developed in the early '80's, evolved from the system of break bulk steamers which were formerly used. The idea was appropriated about a quarter of a century ago by the Trans-Siberian Railroad to cross Lake Baikal.

The Pere Marquette Railway operates seven steamers on this route the year round. It has the special advantage of avoiding the crowded terminals of Chicago, Toledo and Detroit, and is also the most direct and expeditious line between the Northwestern States and the Niagara Frontier. This circumstance was emphasized particularly by the government in the routing of considerable freight during the Great War period. On the preceding pages of this publication appears the tariff applying to the transportation of passengers and automobiles, motorcycles and motor trucks between Manitowoc and Ludington.

In the mid-to-late 1920s, the Pere Marquette Railroad began to promote its ferry fleet more aggressively. With new ships being added, the railroad began to focus on tourism and the revenue it generated. Greater emphasis was placed on food service and public facilities such as lounge space, staterooms, and deck chairs. In an appeal to both freight customers and the burgeoning passenger trade, advertisements like this one were run in freight trade and tourist publications. This particular ad appeared in a 1927 PM vacation guide, but the graphics were likely composed much earlier. All of the scenes show *Pere Marquettes 15* and *17* no later than 1905. (Author's collection.)

Among the new ships to be added were the *Pere Marquettes 21* and *22*. They were built in 1924 by the Manitowoc Shipbuilding Company. Measuring 360 feet long overall, the pair was similar to Robert Logan's ferries but had more powerful triple-expansion steam engines. Their operating speed was 14 miles per hour, compared to the 12 miles per hour standard of the Logan ferries. Pere Marquette 22 is shown entering Kewaunee sometime after her cabin lengthening in 1936. (Author's collection.)

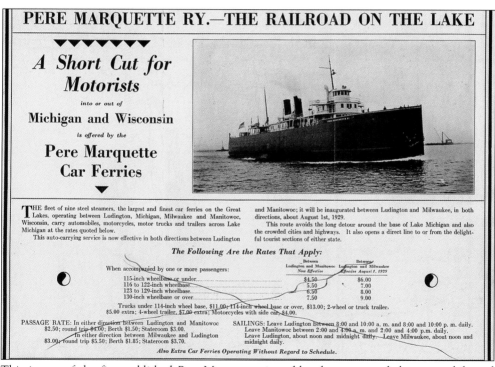

This is one of the first published Pere Marquette timetables that promoted the automobile and passenger trade, c. 1929. With the arrival of two new turbo-electric car ferries capable of traveling at 18 miles per hour, automobile service to Milwaukee was slated to begin around August 1, 1929. As a rule, the PM had always carried autos as space dictated, with railcars taking precedent. This, however, was PM's first attempt at maintaining regularly-scheduled sailings. Noted at the bottom are two-hour windows for departure times. (Author's collection.)

Manitowoc Shipbuilding Company again built a new pair of ferries for the newly reorganized Pere Marquette Railway. The *City of Saginaw 31* entered service in 1929, followed by her twin, the *City of Flint 32*, a year later. Their propulsion system was unlike anything seen on the Lake Michigan car ferries. They utilized steam turbines connected to direct drive electric motors, pushing the twin-screw ships along at a speed of 18 miles per hour. This 1930s-era advertisement shows the mahogany interior of passenger-oriented accommodations of the *Saginaw* and *Flint*. At this time, the PM Railway began to name its new ships after major cities along the road's main line. The previous ships were given numbers with the "*Pere Marquette*" prefix. To recognize the change in propulsion system, the railroad adopted a new series of numbers preceded by the new "*City of*" prefix. (Author's collection.)

The *City of Flint 32* enters Ludington harbor after a run to Milwaukee c. mid-1930s. The *Saginaw* and *Flint* had a refined profile. A large single stack replaced the small twin stacks of their predecessors, and the pair's raised forecastles gave them an appearance suggestive of their speed and power. Their turbo-electric propulsion system was never duplicated in subsequent PM ships, despite its high regard by the fleet's engineers. The design had a high installation cost and was expensive to maintain. (Courtesy Robert Strauss Collection.)

The Pere Marquette Railway took great pride in developing a passenger service second to none among Great Lakes ferry operators. The railroad recruited chefs and dining service staff from some of the finest restaurants in New York and Chicago. During the busy summer vacation months, college students were employed as cabin maids, waiters, cooks, and porters. A few veterans are among this group of fresh-faced school kids shown aboard the *Saginaw* or *Flint*, c. the late 1930s. (Courtesy Mason County Historical Society.)

PERE MARQUETTE

The front of this 1938 menu features a stylized drawing of the *Saginaw/Flint* car ferries. Pere Marquette's publicity department began employing talented graphic artists to illustrate various forms of railroad and ferry-oriented advertising. Much of it reflected the optimistic art deco styling that was prevalent during the 1930s. The car ferries were a high-profile division of the PM Railway, and their likeness adorned everything from soap labels, pens, and matchbooks to posters, china, and billboards. (Courtesy John P. Praedel Collection.)

The dinner menu offered a nice selection of main entrée and a la carte items. Similar variety was found in the printed lunch and breakfast menus. Car ferry crews have always eaten well. Food was simple and plain, but always served in abundance. Their situation improved when the enhanced passenger services were established. Crews were able to order meals from the passenger menus, which translated to higher quality and better selection. (Courtesy John P. Praedel Collection.)

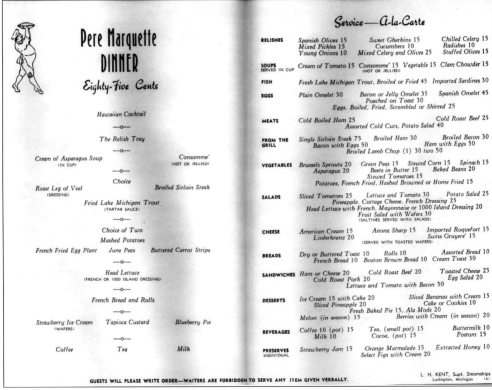

THE QUEEN OF THE LAKES

THE CITY OF MIDLAND, newest addition to the Pere Marquette fleet of steel ships that transport freight trains, automobiles and passengers across Lake Michigan, is now operating in regular service.

Length 406 feet, beam 57 feet, this new steamer has a loaded draft of 17½ feet and a displacement of approximately 8,200 tons. Above her hull, with its steel bulkheads and eleven water-tight safety compartments, the superstructure reveals the graceful lines of modern marine streamlining.

Inside and out, the CITY OF MIDLAND is a ship of beauty and enormous utility, accommodating 34 railroad freight cars on the four tracks of the main car deck and 50 automobiles on the upper deck.

The CITY OF MIDLAND takes leadership as the largest, safest and fastest ship engaged in transporting loaded freight cars, automobiles, and passengers across the timesaving water "bridge" between Ludington, Mich., and the ports of Milwaukee, Manitowoc and Kewaunee, on the Wisconsin side of Lake Michigan.

PERE MARQUETTE RAILWAY

The Railroad That Crosses Lake Michigan

The *City of Midland 41* was the pride of the PM fleet and one of the most popular passenger ships to ever sail the Great Lakes. The 18-mile-per-hour ship was built in 1941 by the Manitowoc Shipbuilding Company. This advertisement says it all. (Author's collection.)

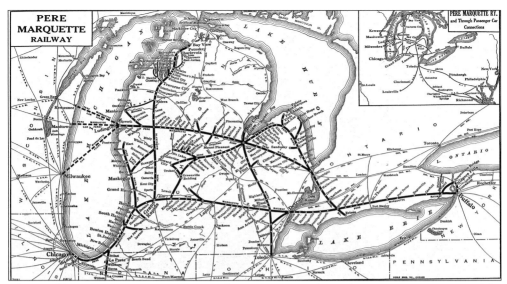

This World War II–era Pere Marquette Railway system map shows the strategic importance of the railroad in its proximity to the industrial heart of the Midwest. The PM's Lake Michigan Fleet as well as its Detroit River ferry operation handled huge quantities of material necessary in the war effort. During the war years, the car ferries ran unimpeded around the clock and year-round. (Author's collection.)

Pere Marquette is on the VICTORY BEAM!

STRAIGHT across Lake Michigan flash the two-way radio waves of Pere Marquette, as ships talk to shore. And in just as straight a line the great Carferries sail . . . carrying full trains of freight cars . . . "on the beam"—and no wasting time on roundabout routes!

In an all-out war, *every short cut counts* . . . and here's a short cut that lops many miles and hours off the schedule of commercial and military freight shipments between the Northwest and the East. At Ludington, Michigan,

and at Milwaukee, Manitowoc and Kewaunee, Wisconsin, loaded freight cars are switched onto the deck tracks of these great steamers. In a few hours they're on the other side . . . ready to continue their journey on the main line. There's no breaking bulk at either shore. And there's no time wasted by detouring around through congested areas. Daily service takes freight across Pere Marquette's "water bridge" . . . saving hours that bring America's victory closer!

13

This Pere Marquette "propaganda" ad appeared in a 1942 system timetable. The PM ferries contributed to the cause by training coast guard recruits on the basics of seamanship. Classes were held in 60-day intervals aboard each ship, with the recruits bunking in passenger staterooms or extra crews' quarters. The *City of Midland 41's* crew also trained US Navy and Royal Navy engineering officers on the operation of the Skinner Unaflow engine. The *Midland's* engines were nearly identical to those found aboard the US Navy's "baby flat-top" CVE aircraft carrier fleet. (Author's collection.)

Capt. Charles A. Robertson brought the new *City of Midland 41* out of the Manitowoc shipyard in 1941. He had done the same during the inaugural trips of the *Pere Marquette 21* in 1924 and the *City of Saginaw 31* in 1929. (His son, Capt. Bernard A. Robertson, would carry on the family tradition when the *Badger* set out on her maiden trip in 1953.) Noted for his exceptional "seat-of-the-pants" seamanship, Captain Robertson got his start with the Ann Arbor car ferries. Pere Marquette's marine superintendent, W.L. Mercereau, was well aware of Robertson's reputation and convinced him to leave the Ann Arbor in 1917. Soon after joining the PM, he became the fleet captain. He is shown near the end of his career, which was cut short by his sudden death in 1944. This portrait was taken at the time the *Midland* came out in 1941. (Courtesy Capt. Bernard Robertson Collection.)

The *City of Midland 41* exceeded the expectations of her owners, who would have ordered an identical boat had the onset of World War II not interfered. Because of wartime shipbuilding restrictions, only military craft were in production at the time; commercial ship construction at Manitowoc would not resume until 1945. The *Midland* is shown during her maiden voyage on March 12, 1941. (Courtesy Wisconsin Maritime Museum at Manitowoc.)

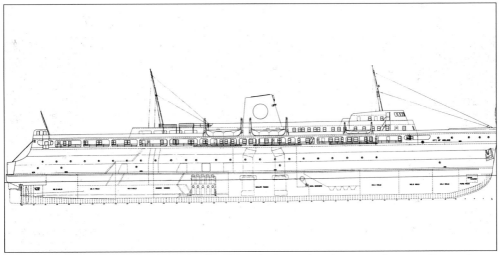

Much was made of the *Midland's* streamlined profile during her first year of service. Press releases were widely distributed by PM Railway's publicity department, all of them touting her unique design aesthetic. She was also the first Great Lakes car ferry to be fitted with two passenger decks, which included an auto storage garage, as well as an open promenade on her cabin deck. She was designed by Andrew M. Houston of the Manitowoc Shipbuilding Company and Leland H. Kent, who replaced W.L. Mercereau as PM's marine superintendent in 1931. (Courtesy Bay Shipbuilding Company.)

New Pere Marquette Car Ferry City of Midland, Ludington, Mich.

The *Midland* was the last ship built by the Pere Marquette Railway. In 1947 the expansive Chesapeake & Ohio Railroad fully absorbed the PM, which had been an affiliate of the railroad's system since 1929. Thereafter, the PM and its marine division became known as the C&O's "Pere Marquette district." Almost immediately, the C&O had plans to improve its newly acquired Lake Michigan car ferry fleet. This post card shows the *Midland* entering Ludington on her maiden voyage. (Author's collection.)

Two

CONSTRUCTION AND
LAUNCHING
1950–1952

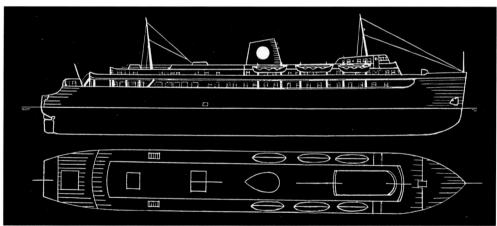

As part of the Chesapeake & Ohio Railroad's fleet improvement program, plans were drawn for at least one, but possibly two new car ferries, contingent upon financing arrangements. Initial plans were laid out by L.H. Kent, based upon the success of his earlier collaboration on the *City of Midland 41*. As this profile sketch suggests, the new ferry class embodied many of the *Midland's* design elements. Compare this with the outboard profile on page 26. Some of these features were eventually dropped, particularly the *Midland*-style pilothouse and stack. However, the new gravity davits were retained, which freed up deck space with their high-mounted lifeboat cradles. These were an improvement over the traditional quadrantal davits, which required the lifeboats to rest on deck level. (Courtesy Andrew LaBorde Collection.)

The Christy Corporation of Sturgeon Bay, Wisconsin, was the successful bidder for the C&O car ferry project. The firm's president, Carl "Ray" Christianson, secured the contract by persuading C&O officials to purchase the materials and equipment and furnish it to the shipyard at cost. This eliminated some of the yard's financing costs and saved C&O ten percent on the cost of its ship. Hull No. 369 is shown under construction in the spring of 1951. (Courtesy Door County Maritime Museum, Photo by Herb Reynolds.)

Ray Christianson's cost-cutting methods allowed the C&O Railway to exercise its option on a second car ferry. The twin ships were initially known simply as Hull Numbers 369 and 370. After several Michigan and Wisconsin communities lobbied to have the ferries named in honor of their cities, C&O management instead named the ferries *Spartan* and *Badger*. They reasoned that by naming the new ships after universities, fewer egos would be bruised. (Courtesy Door County Maritime Museum, Photo by Herb Reynolds.)

Construction of the *Spartan* and *Badger* was delayed by material shortages and cost overruns as a result of the Korean War. Christy Corporation would likely have defaulted on its construction bonds taken on for the car ferry job. Fortunately, a contract for the construction of several naval vessels provided the firm the liquidity to finish both projects. The *Spartan* is seen here on launch day, January 4, 1952. (Courtesy Door County Maritime Museum, Photo by Herb Reynolds.)

Yard personnel clear ice out between the *Spartan's* launchways on January 4, 1952. The ship was launched without ceremonial fanfare; her owners opted for a double christening ceremony during the *Badger's* late summer launching that September. The ship's hull framing and plating were exceptionally heavy to resist mid-winter ice. (Courtesy Door County Maritime Museum, Photo by Herb Reynolds.)

PROGRAM

Launching

S. S. BADGER

Christening

S. S. SPARTAN

September 6, 1952

for

The Chesapeake & Ohio Railway Co.
CLEVELAND, OHIO

The dual car ferry christening ceremony was the culmination of a tremendous achievement carried out by the Christy Corporation. It placed a huge spotlight on the efforts of Ray Christianson and his business partners. They bought the assets of their former employer, the Leathem D. Smith Shipbuilding Company, after Mr. Smith drowned with three other people in a boating accident on Green Bay in 1946. After quite a struggle to pool their resources and secure financing, they established the Christy Corporation in March 1947. The C&O car ferry contract was the largest project the fledgling firm undertook, and the two ships remain a testament to their skill.

Ray Christianson took the podium on September 6, 1952, and stated, "We are certain these ships will do credit to the owners, builders, architects and, of course, the workmen. Without them, the work of the architects would be of no avail. I would like to pay a special tribute to all of the workers of the Christy Corporation." (Both, the author's collection.)

Christening Program
Eleven o'Clock in the Morning

S. S. BADGER

Invocation .... The Rev. Wm. V. Carpenter
Christ The King Episcopal Church, Sturgeon Bay

Remarks .... C. R. Christianson
President, Christy Corporation

Remarks .... W. J. Tuohy
President, The Chesapeake & Ohio Railway Company

Remarks .... LeRoy Luberg
Assistant to President, University of Wisconsin

Remarks .... Governor Walter J. Kohler, Jr.
Governor, State of Wisconsin

Christening .... Mrs. Walter J. Kohler, Jr
Wife of the Governor, State of Wisconsin

S. S. SPARTAN

Invocation .... The Rev. Wm. V. Carpenter
Christ The King Episcopal Church, Sturgeon Bay

Remarks .... C. R. Christianson
President, Christy Corporation

Remarks .... W. J. Tuohy
President, The Chesapeake & Ohio Railway Company

Remarks .... Dr. John A. Hannah
President, Michigan State College

Christening .... Mrs. John A. Hannah
Wife of the President, Michigan State College

Music by Green Bay Packer Band

Mrs. Walter J. Kohler, Jr.

Mrs. John A. Hannah

The launching party stands in front of the *Spartan's* bow in Sturgeon Bay on September 6, 1952. They are, from left to right, Rev. William V. Carpenter, Dr. John A. Hannah (president, Michigan State College), Mrs. Hannah (sponsor of the *Spartan*), C&O's Pres. Walter J. Tuohy, Mrs. C. Ray Christianson, C. Ray Christianson (president, Christy Corporation), Mrs. Walter J. Kohler (sponsor of the *Badger*), and Mr. Walter J. Kohler (governor of Wisconsin). (Courtesy Wisconsin Maritime Museum at Manitowoc, photo by Herb Reynolds.)

Pictured on the *Badger's* launch platform are, from left to right, C&O president Walter J. Tuohy, Wisconsin governor Walter J. Kohler, Mrs. Kohler, and C&O marine superintendent L.H. Kent. (Courtesy Wisconsin Maritime Museum at Manitowoc, photo by Herb Reynolds.)

With the Wisconsin state flag flying from her steering pole, the *Badger* rests on the launchways just hours before her christening on September 6, 1952. Note the shape of her icebreaking prow. (Author's collection, photo by Herb Reynolds.)

Christy Corporation's 250-man launching crew drives 4,000 18-inch-long wooden wedges to raise the *Badger*'s hull off the keelblocks. By raising her hull just a few inches, the ship's weight is transferred to the outbound timber supports of the launch ways. When the entire pre-launch procedure was completed, all that was restraining the ship were eight three-inch hawsers. When the signal was given, pneumatic guillotines cut the lines and gravity forced the *Badger* down the ways. (Courtesy Door County Maritime Museum, photo by Herb Reynolds.)

With the traditional pronouncement of "I christen thee the SS *Badger*," Mrs. Kohler cracks a bottle of champagne across the ship's prow. C&O president Walter J. Tuohy and Wisconsin governor Walter J. Kohler look on. (Courtesy Door County Maritime Museum, photo by Herb Reynolds.)

At 11:17 a.m. on September 6, 1952, the car ferry *Badger* slid down the launchways and into the waters of Sturgeon Bay. The launching was perfect; the only glitch was slight damage to a warehouse caused by the huge wave generated as the ship hit the water. (Courtesy Door County Maritime Museum, photo by Herb Reynolds.)

As the *Badger* slides down the launchways, several shipyard employees are seen standing on the ship's open car deck, tightly clutching a handhold. These men volunteered to go along for the ride and were given the task of handling lines and securing the ship after she settled down. (Courtesy Door County Maritime Museum, photo by Herb Reynolds.)

The *Badger* rolls heavily back on her port side as a wall of water rushes along the warehouse, visible in the background. Old railroad cars and steel plates were placed for protection along the property across from the launch site. (Courtesy Door County Maritime Museum, photo by Herb Reynolds.)

Looking on with pride in the foreground at left, Christy shipyard personnel watch as their creation hits the water. The 410-foot *Badger* slid down the ways in a matter of seconds, but the existing photos show that it was a sight to behold. All of the *Badger* and *Spartan's* builder's photos were the work of the Herb Reynolds Photography Studio of Sturgeon Bay. His firm supplied Christy Corporation, C&O's publicity department, as well as the associated press with the official photos. The yard was off-limits to the public by order of naval security. (Courtesy Door County Maritime Museum, photo by Herb Reynolds.)

The *Badger* settles down after her rush from the launchways. Mooring lines are visible to the right of the ship, as is the containment boom surrounding the slip. This prevented timber shoring and debris from the launching from drifting into the navigation channel in Sturgeon Bay. (Courtesy Door County Maritime Museum, photo by Herb Reynolds.)

This scene shows some of the damage caused by what the press called the *Badger's* "mini-tidal wave." Derelict boxcars were placed with sandbags and steel plating alongside the shipyard's shop warehouse in anticipation of the wave. The cables securing the cars were snapped, and the tremendous force toppled several of them. Damage was slight, amounting to $1,500. (Courtesy Door County Maritime Museum, photo by Herb Reynolds.)

Immediately following the *Badger's* launch, a ceremony was held to christen the nearly completed *Spartan*, launched the previous winter. Dr. John A. Hannah reads a prepared speech in honor of his school's mascot being selected as the ship's namesake. At left, his wife stands at the ready, champagne bottle in hand. (Courtesy Door County Maritime Museum, photo by Herb Reynolds.)

Mrs. John A. Hannah and C&O marine superintendent L.H. Kent get drenched with champagne as the bottle hits its mark across the *Spartan's* bow. Honor students representing the University of Wisconsin and Michigan State College were in attendance during the ceremonies and luncheon. They served as the sponsors' courts of honor. (Courtesy Door County Maritime Museum, photo by Herb Reynolds.)

A representative of Herb Reynolds Photography took this excellent overhead photo of the *Spartan's* christening. The moment was captured perfectly as the champagne flies and a photographer's flash bulb reflects off the ship's gleaming hull. (Courtesy Door County Maritime Museum, photo by Herb Reynolds.)

A happy group of onlookers cheer in approval at the conclusion of the ceremonies. The event was closed to the public and only invited guests and the shipyard employees were admitted. The yard was in control of a naval security detachment during the construction of five US Navy LSTs. (Courtesy Door County Maritime Museum, photo by Herb Reynolds.)

A post-ceremonial luncheon and tour were held aboard the nearly completed *Spartan*. To accommodate the large guest list, the ship's car deck railroad tracks were planked over for the event. Ray Christianson is shown presenting a gift box to both of the christening sponsors, Mrs. Hannah, left, and Mrs. Kohler, right. The cost of the event was paid entirely by the Chesapeake & Ohio Railway, including food and beverage service, table and chair rental, and the time-consuming process of planking over the car deck. In his memoirs, Ray Christianson recalled that the C&O paid his firm over $25,000 for their part in planking and general preparation of the *Spartan*. Given the success of the day's events, it was money well spent. (Courtesy Door County Maritime Museum, photo by Herb Reynolds.)

Three

SEA TRIALS AND DELIVERY
1952–1953

The *Spartan* was ready for her sea trials on September 27, 1952. The first of the twin car ferries is shown passing between the highway 42 bridge in Sturgeon Bay, Wisconsin. She is shown headed east down the ship canal toward the waters of Lake Michigan. She is about to undergo a rigorous battery of tests to prove to her owners, builders, and the government inspectors that she is a seaworthy craft. Sea trials were also known as the owner's trials, acceptance trials, or more commonly, the "shakedown cruise." (Author's collection.)

The *Spartan* begins a high-speed turn during her sea trials. When pushed to their limits, the *Spartan* and *Badger* attained a maximum speed of 24 miles per hour during these tests. Modifications to the engines' steam super-heaters and a labor strike by C&O car ferry crews delayed the *Spartan's* delivery. (Author's collection, photo by Herb Reynolds.)

Commercial photographer Herb Reynolds occasionally chartered an airplane to capture aerial photos of ships undergoing trials off the Door County peninsula. In this view the *Spartan* heads south along the Wisconsin coast, September 27, 1952. She was delivered to her owners on October 23rd. (Author's collection, photo by Herb Reynolds.)

The *Badger* was ready for her sea trials on March 16, 1953. She is shown while conducting anchor tests off Kewaunee, Wisconsin. This black and white post card was distributed free of charge to passengers as they boarded the ship during her first year of service. (Author's collection.)

During her trials, the *Badger* was crowded by scores of engineers and equipment representatives. All had a common interest in ensuring that their machinery passed muster during the testing and inspection process. L.A. Offar collects boiler performance data from the general regulator control panel for the ship's owners. (Courtesy Capt. Bernard Robertson Collection.)

This was a typical scene throughout the ship as technicians charted the operational characteristics of their equipment. This view was taken in the ship's windlass room. (Courtesy Capt. Bernard Robertson Collection.)

The *Badger* is shown completing her anchor tests and is ready to get underway. One of the most dramatic tests conducted that day was the emergency stop/collision-avoidance test. As the ship was proceeding at her full 18-mph speed, Captain Robertson stopped his engines and immediately threw the control indicators to full-speed reverse. Within 1400 feet and an elapsed time of two minutes and ten seconds the *Badger* shuddered to a halt. At full speed the engines were turning over at 120 revolutions per minute. They took eight seconds to stop and 16 additional seconds to get them to 100 revolutions per minute full-speed astern. (Courtesy Capt. Bernard Robertson Collection.)

Her anchor tests completed, the *Badger* turns around to resume her performance testing and to pose for publicity photos with her sister ship, the *Spartan*. This view was taken from the Wisconsin Department of Natural Resources research vessel *Barney Devine* off Kewaunee harbor. (Courtesy John W. Hausmann, photo by Herb Reynolds.)

Owen Wanke of Sturgeon Bay throws a wooden block overboard from the area known as the "winch well" located in the *Badger's* forecastle. Blocks were thrown over the side so that the ship's course could be observed during turning maneuvers. It is unclear if these markers were ever recovered from the lake. (Courtesy Capt. Bernard Robertson Collection.)

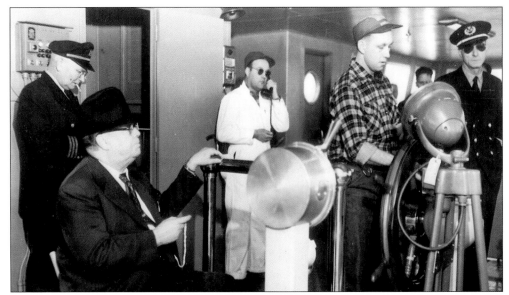

The *Badger's* pilothouse was the center of activity during the collision-avoidance test. From left to right are the first mate Ed Halden, C&O marine superintendent L.H. Kent, secretary of the Christy Corporation B.J. Lienau, wheelsman Glen Bentz, and Capt. Bernard Robertson. With stopwatch in hand, L.H. Kent was the official timekeeper for many of the day's activities. (Courtesy Capt. Bernard Robertson Collection.)

In between her testing, the *Badger* came into Kewaunee harbor to be fitted to the railcar loading apron and to take on several coal cars to fuel her bunkers. This excellent photo was taken from the *Badger's* car deck upon her arrival. The *Spartan* dominates the background as she loads in Kewaunee's north slip. (Courtesy Capt. Bernard Robertson Collection.)

The *Badger* takes on her first load of fuel at Kewaunee, March 16, 1953. Like all of the C&O car ferries and their predecessors, they were coal-fired steamships. Because the C&O Railway was a major coal-hauling road, the coal and its transportation costs were inexpensive. This was the reason the *Spartan* and *Badger* were not built with diesel engines. (Courtesy Wisconsin Maritime Museum at Manitowoc.)

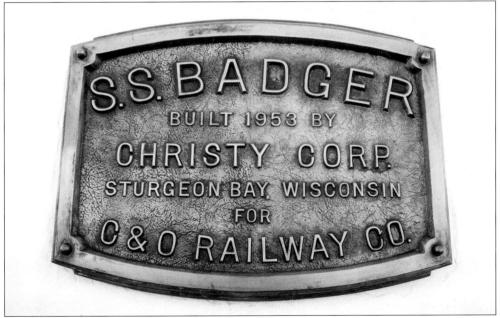

The Chesapeake & Ohio and the Christy shipyard worked closely in cross-promoting the *Badger* for publicity purposes. The ship's prominently-displayed bronze builder's plate reflects this cooperation. There were actually three builders' plates on both the *Badger* and *Spartan*. One was located on the forward superstructure beneath the pilothouse, one was mounted near the stern on the aft end of the passenger cabin, and one was located in the engine room. (Photo by Max Hanley.)

A carhandler tightens a wheel clamp on a coal hopper during the ship's stopover at Kewaunee. The car ferries railcar cargo was secured during heavy weather by a system of screw jacks, chains (to prevent tipping), and wheel clamps (to prevent rolling). Fair weather prevailed that day, but the fuel cars were nevertheless jacked up as a precaution. The *Badger* took on heavy lists during her emergency turning maneuvers later that afternoon, which could have conceivably turned the cars over onto their sides. (Courtesy Capt. Bernard Robertson Collection.)

The *Badger*, left, and the *Spartan* all but fill the tiny harbor at Kewaunee. Two Green Bay & Western Railroad Alco locomotives are visible loading up the *Badger's* fuel cars. Within moments, the twin ships would head out into the lake to maneuver for publicity photos. (Courtesy Capt. Bernard Robertson Collection, photo by Herb Reynolds.)

For a short period of time the *Badger* carried the homeport of Milwaukee on the seagate at her stern. This was a formality, as she was primarily financed by the Northwestern Mutual Life Insurance Company of Milwaukee. Only upon the ship's official delivery to her owners, and after the transfer of the ship's documentation, would the name "Ludington" replace "Milwaukee." The *Spartan* had a similar arrangement the previous year. (Courtesy Wisconsin Maritime Museum at Manitowoc, photo by Herb Reynolds.)

This is by far the most widely distributed publicity photo of C&O's twin car ferries. This view has appeared on post cards, wall posters, in newspapers and magazines, and has graced the covers of two books. The *Badger*, at the top of the photo (the cleaner of the two ships), would soon break away to finish her trials, while the *Spartan* continued on with her cargo to Ludington. (Courtesy Capt. Bernard Robertson Collection, photo by Herb Reynolds.)

Railroad and paper industry executives gather on the loading apron as the *Badger's* maiden cargo is pushed aboard. Captain Robertson stands at center; second from the right, front row, in the dark hat is superintendent L.H. Kent; and at the far right, back row, is Kent's assistant marine superintendent, Theodor Winkel. (Courtesy Capt. Bernard Robertson Collection.)

This view was taken just prior to the *Badger's* maiden voyage on March 21, 1953. She lies awaiting her cargo in Manitowoc's west lakefront slip. On the left, barely visible in the east slip, is the *Ann Arbor No. 5*. The *Badger* left Manitowoc at 3:30 p.m. and arrived amid great fanfare at Ludington shortly after 7:00 p.m. (Courtesy Wayne Bailey Collection.)

In this view taken from the *Badger's* stern upper deck, Capt. Bernard Robertson greets invited guests aboard his ship the day after the maiden voyage. Public and private tours were held aboard ship on Sunday, March 22, at Ludington. (Courtesy Capt. Bernard Robertson Collection.)

Captain Robertson (center) greets freight shippers and railroad executives prior to a post-maiden voyage luncheon held in the ship's dining room. Looking on to the right of Robertson is C&O dining representative Ray Lessard (with hand in pocket) and the ship's steward, Frank Gorzynski. (Courtesy Capt. Bernard Robertson Collection.)

After the *Badger's* initial maiden voyage from Manitowoc to Ludington, the C&O Railway held a series of "maiden cargo" voyages from the various ports she served. A group of officials representing the C&O and Kenosha, Wisconsin's Nash automobile plant are shown on the apron at Milwaukee's Jones Island ferry slip. (Author's collection.)

The Green Bay & Western Railroad got into the act at the road's "Kewaunee Gateway." The railroad's officials pose with representatives from Green Bay, Wisconsin's paper mills. Paper products were a major eastbound freight commodity out of the ports of Manitowoc and Kewaunee. (Author's collection.)

An unusual solid cargo of tractors on flatcars was loaded during "maiden voyage week" at Jones Island slip, Milwaukee. Notice the lack of business representatives that were present during the daytime voyages. Two of the three men shown are actually part of the railroad switching crew. (Author's collection.)

On Sunday March 22, 1953, a day-long open house tour was held aboard the *Badger* at Ludington. Scores of the city's residents wait patiently in line to board the ship. Thousands took advantage of the opportunity to see the fleet's new flagship. This and the following shipboard tour images were captured by the staff of the *Ludington Daily News*. The newspaper reported that 950 visitors boarded the ship during one half-hour period. (Courtesy Ken Ottmann Collection.)

Many young families, some of them employed by the C&O Railway, enjoyed their tour of the ship. Marine superintendent Kent stands watch at the gangplank as some young boys stumble aboard. The gangplank was normally used for one-way traffic at a given time. (Author's collection.)

A tour group comes down the stairway aft of the *Badger's* outside dining area. An awning protected this area; its heavy framework is visible. In 1960, the stairway was removed and this open area was extended to cover the top of the aft pilothouse (visible on the right) and served as an upper automobile deck when dockside auto ramps were erected. This deck could accommodate between 15 and 18 autos. (Courtesy Ken Ottmann Collection.)

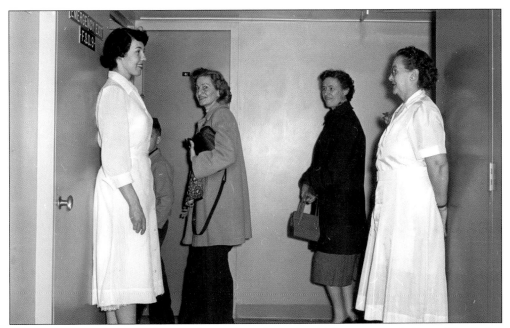

The tour line passes two cabin maids standing along the ship's stateroom hallway. The *Badger* and *Spartan* each had 60 rooms, 44 of which were outside with a window, two beds, a sink, and a toilet. The 16 inside rooms were slightly larger, with a shower, but did not have a window. They were simple and comfortable, well suited for the six-hour Ludington to Milwaukee run. (Author's collection.)

One of the tour's highlights was the ship's galley. Much was made of the spacious all-stainless steel equipment and the latest in modern appliances. In this scene one of the ship's cooks answers questions asked by young mothers enjoying the tour of the ship. (Author's collection.)

The *Badger's* dining room could accommodate 60 passengers at a time, and was normally used as a full service restaurant. It also could be quickly converted to a buffet-style cafeteria. Capt. Bernard Robertson enjoys a meal with his daughter, Audrey, and wife, Florence, in this view taken during the ship's maiden voyage. (Courtesy Capt. Bernard Robertson Collection.)

The main lounges of the *Badger* and *Spartan* each had the capacity to hold 200 passengers, and their interiors were designed to the specifications of Allan Cripe, of C&O's research consultant's office. Martin-Parry Corporation manufactured the furniture, much of which consisted of imitations of Eero Saarinen's famous "womb chair" and "grasshopper chair" designs.(Courtesy Capt. Bernard Robertson Collection.)

Four

SERVICE HISTORY
C&O AND THE CHESSIE SYSTEM
1953–1983

TWO NEW SHIPS
IN C&O's YEAR-'ROUND FLEET
IMPROVES SERVICE ACROSS LAKE MICHIGAN

THE new Twin Queens of the Lakes—the S.S. Spartan and the S.S. Badger, largest and finest ships of their type in the world, now pace Chesapeake and Ohio Railway's year-round auto ferry fleet in providing improved short-cut service across Lake Michigan for motorists.

Accommodations aboard the new, streamlined vessels are of the latest type for real cruising comfort. Lounging on deck, enjoying good meals in the brilliantly designed dining room and relaxing in the modernly furnished staterooms are pleasant escapes for you and your car from driving strain. Enjoy a restful "break" while traveling on the time-saving water "highways" between Ludington, gateway to West Michigan, and the Wisconsin ports of Milwaukee, Manitowoc and and Kewaunee.

Automobiles are loaded and unloaded at ports by C&O steamer personnel. For folders and information apply to your nearest A.A.A. Office or C&O Railway Ticket Office. Confirmed advance reservations recommended for automobile passage.

CHESAPEAKE AND OHIO RAILWAY

As this ad attests, the *Badger* and *Spartan* quickly proved to the C&O the wisdom of their investment in their recently-acquired Lake Michigan ferry fleet. The ships fit in well with their freight car, auto, and passenger capacity. The pair were kept on the Ludington to Milwaukee run during the busy summer tourist season months. During this time the railroad further enhanced its fleet by putting new boilers and Skinner engines into the *Pere Marquettes 21* and *22*. These engines were similarly configured but slightly smaller than those on the *Badger* and *Spartan*. The *21* and *22* were also lengthened 40 feet, allowing each ship to carry four additional railcars per trip. (Author's collection.)

The *Spartan* is shown at Milwaukee's Maple Street slip c. 1957. The passenger waiting room and ticket office were built around 1955. Note the covered walkway between the building and the ship's gangplank. Passengers and autos boarded at both the Maple Street and Jones Island slips in Milwaukee. To expedite scheduling and consolidate Milwaukee operations, the Maple Street facilities were closed at the end of the 1960 summer season. (Photo by Jim Scribbins.)

As a child, Ken Ottmann of Milwaukee would frequently sail out of the Maple Street dock with his mother and aunts enroute to visit relatives in Manistee, Michigan. While standing on the *Spartan's* bow during one of these trips, a crewman noticed young Kenny gazing up at the pilothouse. He called down and asked him if he would like to come up. The result was a tour of the ship's bridge and the thrill of getting to steer the ship. Kenny's only regret that exciting day was that he was not aboard his favorite ship, the *Badger*. (Courtesy Ken Ottmann Collection.)

Capt. Bernard Robertson enjoys one of the benefits of being skipper of C&O's flagship. In 1960, these professional models accompanied a film crew aboard the *Badger*. They were part of the production of C&O's 16-mm Lake Michigan car ferry promotional film, *The Golden Link*. A still photographer also captured images for C&O's printed materials, such as timetables and annual reports. This photo was taken at the engine control telegraph station in the *Badger's* pilothouse. (Courtesy Capt. Bernard Robertson Collection.)

This rare photo shows the *Badger* heading down the Kinnickinnic River just after departing Milwaukee's Maple Street slip. The white gate marks the end of the loading apron and at the right is the covered passenger stairway and gangplank. This image was taken on September 20, 1956. (Courtesy Capt. Bernard Robertson Collection, photo by Les Borst.)

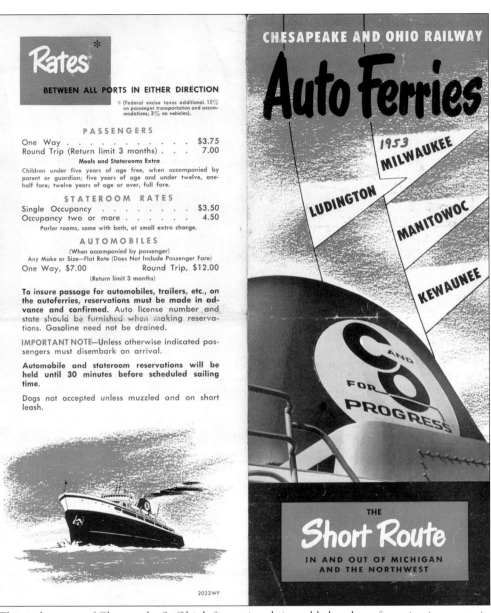

Rates *

BETWEEN ALL PORTS IN EITHER DIRECTION

* (Federal excise taxes additional. 15% on passenger transportation and accommodations; 3% on vehicles).

PASSENGERS

One Way $3.75
Round Trip (Return limit 3 months) . . . 7.00

Meals and Staterooms Extra

Children under five years of age free, when accompanied by parent or guardian; five years of age and under twelve, one-half fare; twelve years of age or over, full fare.

STATEROOM RATES

Single Occupancy $3.50
Occupancy two or more 4.50

Parlor rooms, some with bath, at small extra charge.

AUTOMOBILES

(When accompanied by passenger)
Any Make or Size—Flat Rate (Does Not Include Passenger Fare)

One Way, $7.00   Round Trip, $12.00

(Return limit 3 months)

To insure passage for automobiles, trailers, etc., on the autoferries, reservations must be made in advance and confirmed. Auto license number and state should be furnished when making reservations. Gasoline need not be drained.

IMPORTANT NOTE—Unless otherwise indicated passengers must disembark on arrival.

Automobile and stateroom reservations will be held until 30 minutes before scheduled sailing time.

Dogs not accepted unless muzzled and on short leash.

2023WF

CHESAPEAKE AND OHIO RAILWAY

Auto Ferries

1953

LUDINGTON

MILWAUKEE

MANITOWOC

KEWAUNEE

C AND O FOR PROGRESS

THE
Short Route
IN AND OUT OF MICHIGAN AND THE NORTHWEST

This is the cover of Chesapeake & Ohio's first printed timetable brochure featuring its new twin car ferries; the *Badger's* stack is prominent on the right front panel. This was also the first time the railroad's publicity department used its new caricature drawing of the *Badger/Spartan*, shown at the lower part of the left panel. This drawing has been modified over the past fifty years and remains in use today. This schedule is from 1953. (Author's collection.)

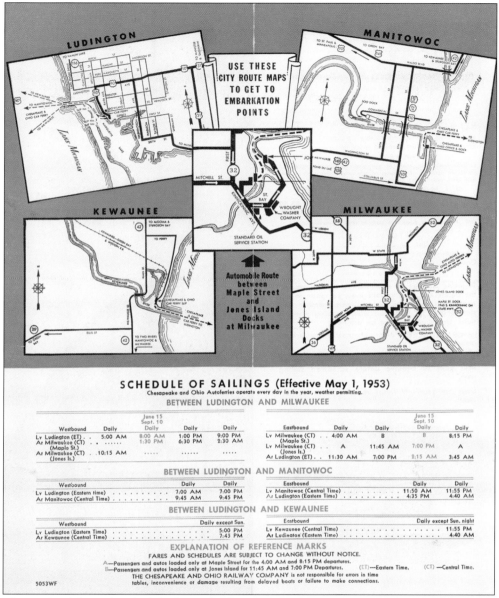

SCHEDULE OF SAILINGS (Effective May 1, 1953)

Chesapeake and Ohio Autoferries operate every day in the year, weather permitting.

BETWEEN LUDINGTON AND MILWAUKEE

	Daily	June 15 Sept. 10 Daily	Daily	Daily		Daily	Daily	June 15 Sept. 10 Daily	Daily
Westbound					Eastbound				
Lv Ludington (ET) . .	5:00 AM	8:00 AM	1:00 PM	9:00 PM	Lv Milwaukee (CT) . . (Maple St.)	4:00 AM	B	B	8:15 PM
Ar Milwaukee (CT) . . (Maple St.)	......	1:30 PM	6:30 PM	2:30 AM	Lv Milwaukee (CT) . . (Jones Is.)	A	11:45 AM	7:00 PM	A
Ar Milwaukee (CT) . .10:15 AM (Jones Is.)		......	......	......	Ar Ludington (ET). .	11:30 AM	7:00 PM	2:15 AM	3:45 AM

BETWEEN LUDINGTON AND MANITOWOC

		Daily	Daily			Daily	Daily
Westbound				Eastbound			
Lv Ludington (Eastern time)	. . . .	7:00 AM	7:00 PM	Lv Manitowoc (Central Time)	. . . .	11:50 AM	11:55 PM
Ar Manitowoc (Central Time)	. . . .	9:45 AM	9:45 PM	Ar Ludington (Eastern time)	. . . .	4:35 PM	4:40 AM

BETWEEN LUDINGTON AND KEWAUNEE

		Daily except Sun.			Daily except Sun. night
Westbound			Eastbound		
Lv Ludington (Eastern time)	. . . .	5:00 PM	Lv Kewaunee (Central Time)	. . . .	11:55 PM
Ar Kewaunee (Central Time)	. . . .	7:45 PM	Ar Ludington (Eastern time)	. . . .	4:40 AM

EXPLANATION OF REFERENCE MARKS

FARES AND SCHEDULES ARE SUBJECT TO CHANGE WITHOUT NOTICE.

A—Passengers and autos loaded only at Maple Street for the 4:00 AM and 8:15 PM departures.
B—Passengers and autos loaded only at Jones Island for 11:45 AM and 7:00 PM Departures.   (ET)—Eastern Time.   (CT)—Central Time.
THE CHESAPEAKE AND OHIO RAILWAY COMPANY is not responsible for errors in time tables, inconvenience or damage resulting from delayed boats or failure to make connections.

5053WF

The inside of the 1953 schedule shows the different car ferry docks and the street map between Milwaukee's two ferry slips. The schedule of sailings list, somewhat difficult to read, was made all the more vexing by the "A" and "B" reference marks denoting the Maple Street and Jones Island departures. More than a few people arrived at the wrong slip, only to see their ship sailing away once they drove around the long harbor peninsula to the correct embarkation point. (Author's collection.)

The hull and stack livery in this photo was worn by the *Badger* from 1961 until late 1973. This is the longest-lived of any of the many variations of paint schemes. Note how the stack colors are now reversed to light lettering on a dark background (yellow on blue). Her hull stripes from top to bottom are white, black, white, and black. When she first came out, the colors from top to bottom were white, grey, white, and black. (Photo by John W. Hausmann.)

The *Badger* takes on a load of freight cars at Milwaukee's Jones Island ferry slip. This facility was opened in 1929 and leased to C&O's predecessor, the Pere Marquette Railway. This view was taken in 1960 from the recently-erected ramp that led to the ship's upper auto deck, added only a few months before. (Courtesy Ken Ottmann Collection.)

These are pages of a foldout brochure advertising the promotional C&O Railway film, *The Golden Link*. Produced by Chicago's Fred Niles Productions, the 16-mm film was widely used by the railroad's traffic department to persuade freight shippers to use its ferry service. Depending on the intended audience, C&O's marketing department began calling its ships "trainferries" and "autoferries" sometime around 1960. (Courtesy Tom Read Collection.)

This night view shows the *Badger* having a load of freight removed at Jones Island in November 1970. The boxcars in the foreground are headed onto the ship' starboard center track to take off the last cut of cars. (Photo by John W. Hausmann.)

With all the railcars removed, the ship's crew awaits the return of the switch engine with an eastbound load of 26 to 30 cars. During loading operations, the ship's four tracks were referred to as, from left to right; port wing, port center, starboard center, and starboard wing. As freight cars grew longer, the ship's cargo capacity diminished. This reduced capacity and rising labor costs prompted C&O to reevaluate the future of its ferry service during the 1960s and early 1970s. (Photo by John W. Hausmann.)

This view looks toward the *Badger's* starboard (right) side in the forward section of her lounge. The chairs pictured are knock-offs of Eero Saarinen's famous "womb chair" design of 1950. The ship also had similar two-person "settees." (Photo by John W. Hausmann.)

This view looks forward down the *Badger's* port (left) stateroom hallway. There were 60 rooms, 44 facing outside and 16 inside. The narrow corridor did not require handrails for the passengers. In rough weather rolling, all one needed to do was hold his or her arms out to touch both walls. This helped maintain balance and a sense of dignity. (Photo by John W. Hausmann.)

This is the main entry point for passengers boarding the *Badger*, as it appeared in the C&O era. This view faces aft on the port side of the ship's lounge. There was seating capacity for about 200 in this window-lined lounge. (Photo by John W. Hausmann.)

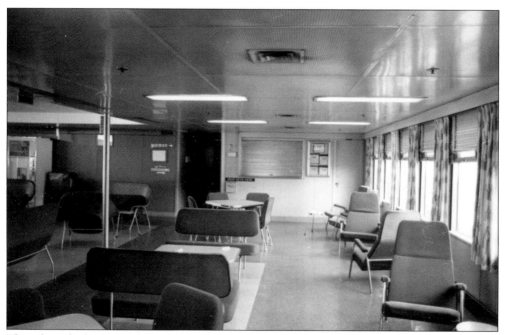

This photo looks forward from the middle of the ship's lounge, starboard side. In the center background is the closed window of the purser's office. From here, one could purchase staterooms, upgrade tickets, and get travel directions. Along the windows to the right are several imitation Eero Saarinen "grasshopper chairs." (Photo by John W. Hausmann.)

C&O maintained Pere Marquette's high standards for excellent shipboard meals. During the summer months extra staff was hired to provide passengers with a full-service dining room. Here John Baron, one of the *Badger's* cooks, prepares dishes of sirloin tips and meatloaf with mashed potatoes and string beans for waiter Walter Schweiger. Note the three-sectioned china plates featuring the ship's logo. (Courtesy Ken Ottmann Collection.)

Pies, cakes, and cookies were made fresh daily on board, and were obviously popular with the crew. Universally, the ship's cook was a highly respected position. A cook with a good reputation was important, as it helped the crew's morale, particularly during the monotonous winter months. First Cook John Vest poses with a sheet of chocolate chip cookies. (Photo by Ken Ottmann.)

Shortly after the *Badger* and *Spartan* came out, several companies that provided equipment used the ferries in a variety of advertisements. One of the most interesting is this ad promoting the ships' use of the Skinner Compound Unaflow engines. These are still in use aboard the *Badger*. See Appendix D, page 152, for design details. (Courtesy Skinner Engine Company, Author's collection.)

During February and March of 1963, nearly the entire navigable surface of Lake Michigan froze over. This created problems for all of the Lake Michigan car ferry operators. The ships were delayed for hours at a time and some even sustained hull and propeller damage. With the prevailing westerly winds, ice tended to pile up on the eastern shore of the lake. Shown here are the *Badger*, at left, with her twin, the *Spartan*, off Ludington harbor. (Photo by Mary DuBrow.)

Shown in Ludington on a much more serene summer afternoon, the *Spartan* takes on a load at left in No. 2 slip, while the *Badger* drops anchor and approaches No. 3 slip. This view was taken in 1977, one of the last years the pair would ever sail together. By this time, the C&O Railway had petitioned the Interstate Commerce Commission to abandon its car ferry service. (Photo by Dan Bissell.)

The *Badger* departs Ludington sporting her bright new "Chessie" in the "C" stack logo. In the early 1970s, the C&O merged with several railroads to form the "Chessie System." The three remaining ships in C&O's fleet received this emblem in time for the 1976 summer passenger season. (Photo by Max Hanley.)

A Chicago & Northwestern locomotive loads the *Badger* at Manitowoc's lakefront slip, c. 1975. During loading operations, railroad flatcars were used as "idler cars" to keep the weight of the heavy switch engines off the loading aprons. If these idlers were not available, such as in Kewaunee, standard railcars would be used in their place. (Photo by John W. Hausmann.)

During rough weather, railroad cars were secured as soon as they were loaded aboard ship. To prevent cars from tipping over during heavy rolls, screw jacks would be inserted and raised under each corner of a car. This would take the car's weight off its springs to eliminate any swaying motion. To counteract the jacks, chains and turnbuckles would be lashed down adjacent to the jack, making the car rigid and almost a part of the ship's deck. Bob Palmer demonstrates the procedure. (Courtesy Mason County Historical Society.)

During any trip, the minimum amount of gear applied to the load of railcars was a set of wheel clamps. These would be placed behind the wheels on the last car of each four strings of cars. In the case of extra-heavy cars, two clamps would be "doubled up" (as shown) to prevent the string of cars from rolling. When jacks, clamps, and chains were employed, this was known as "putting up full gear." High-sided hopper cars were chained down to the deck by means of "top-hooks," secured from the top of the car to long chains on the bottom. (Photo by Ken Ottmann.)

Capt. John F. Bissell was one of the *Badger's* skippers from the late 1970s to the mid-1980s. At the time this photo was taken in 1978, the Chessie System Railroad was proving to the federal government that its ferries were no longer profitable to operate. Railcars could now be routed quickly and efficiently on land via Chicago to points east and west, far cheaper than by car ferry. (Photo by Dan Bissell.)

By the time Chessie's abandonment efforts were well along, its fleet was reduced to three ships. They are shown at Ludington from left to right, the *Badger*, the *City of Midland 41*, and the *Spartan*. The *Pere Marquettes 21* and *22* and the *City of Saginaw 31* were retired from service and sold during the mid-1970s. The *City of Flint 32* had been retired in 1967. (Photo by Dan Bissell.)

Like the winter of 1962–1963, 1976–1977 saw Lake Michigan freeze over from shore to shore. In February 1977, AB watchman Raymond Short photographed this view from atop the Spartan's aft mast as the *Badger* (right) attempts to free her sistership from an ice ridge. In this scene, the *Badger* moves forward alongside and prepares to swing her stern across the Spartan's bow. By creating heavy propeller wash, the ice would loosen up around the ship's hulls. (Photo by Raymond Short.)

The *Badger* lies in Manitowoc's west lakefront slip while the Ann Arbor Railroad's *Viking* occupies the east slip on a cold, icy evening. During the winter months, unscheduled sailings prevailed. Occasionally, at Manitowoc and Kewaunee, the rival Ann Arbor and C&O boats would race each other to reach the harbor first. The ferries were unloaded by one railroad switching crew, so service was provided on a first-come, first-served basis. The slower boat generally ended up in port for three hours at the very least. (Photo by Carl Blahnik.)

The *Spartan* breaks through a thin layer of snow-covered ice in Ludington harbor in February 1977. She would make her last trip at the end of the summer passenger season in September 1979. (Photo by Dan Bissell.)

The *Spartan* passes Ludington's north breakwall lighthouse near the end of her career. In 1978, the Interstate Commerce Commission granted Chessie permission to systematically abolish its ferry routes. Milwaukee was abandoned first in 1980, Manitowoc in 1982, and Kewaunee was to follow suit in 1983 if passenger, auto, and freight traffic figures were not substantially above the 1976 numbers of 159,301, 51,470, and 26,980, respectively. It was a foregone conclusion that the figures would fall far short and that Chessie would soon be out of the car ferry business. (Photo by Dan Bissell.)

The *Badger* lies in No. 2 1/2 slip at Ludington. Every spring or fall the ships would use this slip during their annual inspections. The US Coast Guard would thoroughly examine the ship's engines, boilers, navigational, and safety devices. Every five years, the ships were required to undergo a hull survey, which involved a trip to the shipyard for drydocking. (Photo by Robert Vande Vusse.)

In an effort to bolster summer car ferry patronage, the Ludington Area Chamber of Commerce paid for newspaper advertisements like this one. Since the end was near, Chessie invested little money promoting its cross-lake service. In spite of the car ferries' uncertain future, passenger and automobile traffic always remained high. (Author's collection.)

Purser John Petrovich stands duty at Chessie's Milwaukee Jones Island car ferry dock. The bag hanging below the booth's window contains muzzles, which were required for all dogs roaming the ship's passenger areas. (Photo by Ken Ottmann.)

Trish Ottmann waits for the crowd to thin out before boarding the *Badger* with her husband, Ken. This scene was taken at Milwaukee during the summer of 1981. Large crowds like these were typical. Chessie had abandoned Milwaukee the previous October, but the State of Michigan implemented a summer-only run on a trial basis between June 11th and September 8th, 1981. (Photo by Ken Ottmann.)

CHESSIE SYSTEM SCHEDULE
JUNE 1 — SEPTEMBER 8, 1981
Daily between Ludington, Mich. and Manitowoc and Kewaunee, Wis.

EASTBOUND

Manitowoc to Ludington (disembark on arrival)
Leaves 11:59 AM CDT (noon), arrives 5:00 PM EDT

Kewaunee to Ludington (disembark on arrival)
Leaves 11:59 PM CDT (midnight), arrives 5:00 AM EDT

Automobiles must be at dock two hours before sailing.

WESTBOUND

Ludington to Manitowoc (disembark on arrival)
Leaves 7:00 AM EDT, arrives 10:00 AM CDT

Ludington to Kewaunee (disembark on arrival)
Leaves 7:00 PM EDT, arrives 10:00 PM CDT

STATE OF MICHIGAN SCHEDULE
JUNE 11 — SEPTEMBER 8, 1981
**Daily except Tuesday and Wednesday
Between Ludington, Mich. and Milwaukee, Wis.
(Chessie System Railroads, Agents)**

EASTBOUND

Milwaukee to Ludington
Leaves 3:30 PM CDT, arrives 10:30 PM EDT
(Disembark at Ludington by 7:30 AM EDT next morning)

Automobiles must be at dock two hours before sailing.

WESTBOUND

Ludington to Milwaukee
Leaves 9:00 AM EDT, arrives 2:00 PM CDT
(Disembark at Milwaukee on arrival)

**Confirmed advance reservations
recommended for automobile passage**

FARES

PASSENGER	One Way	Round Trip (5-Day Limit)
Adults	$12.70	$17.80
Children 5-15	$ 6.35	$ 8.90

	One Way
*AUTOMOBILES	$23.10
*Pickup Truck with Camper on top	$29.05
*Motorcycles on own wheels	$23.10
*Bicycles on own wheels	$ 3.75

** TRAILERS

Utility Trailer (Up to 20 feet)	$29.05
House Trailers (LUp to 20 feet)	$43.10
*Motorized Home (Up to 20 feet)	$29.05

(Above vehicles—$6.05 per foot in excess of 20 ft.)
*When accompanied by passengers, passenger fare additional.
**Accompanying vehicle and passengers additional. Unaccompanied vehicles subject to freight tariff. Check with agent.

ACCOMODATIONS

Stateroom, day occupancy	$12.70
Stateroom, night occupancy	$16.30
Parlors (on City of Midland only.)	
Day occupancy	$16.30
Night occupancy	$19.80

(Effective June 1, 1981, subject to approval by the Interstate Commerce Commission)

THE CHESSIE CRUISE PACKAGE—a continuous round-trip without stopover, including one meal—is available on certain sailings. Fares: Adults—$21.20. Children, 5-15—$10.60; under 5, free. Please check with dock agents for details.

CONDITIONS OF PASSAGE

To insure passage for automobiles, trailers, etc., on the Autoferries, reservations should be made in advance and confirmed. Number of persons, auto license number and state should be furnished when making reservations. Gasoline need not be drained. Automobiles are loaded by ship personnel.

Reservations for automobiles and staterooms will be held until one hour before scheduled sailing time, except as noted under Manitowoc sailings, and must be picked up at dock office prior to this time.

Dogs are not permitted unless muzzled and on a short leash. Muzzles are available aboard from the ship's clerk, a small deposit required.

Sailings are subject to change without notice. Chessie System is not responsible for errors in timetables, inconvenience or damage resulting from delayed boats, or failure to make connections. Not responsible for personal property left in automobile or on ship.

**Michigan observes Eastern Daylight Time
Wisconsin observes Central Daylight Time**

In 1981, the State of Michigan, submitting to the pressure of the Ludington-area tourism industry, subsidized the *Badger* on a summer run to Milwaukee. The Chessie System provided the ship and crew, but the operating costs and paychecks were paid for with state funds. The *Badger's* departure and arrival time was more favorable for the westbound passengers. As a concession, eastbound passengers who purchased staterooms were allowed to remain on board overnight. Successful as the run was, the Michigan Department of Transportation did not reinstate the service in 1982. (Author's collection.)

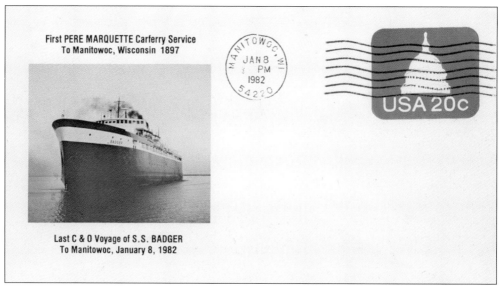

Chessie System abandoned the second of its three routes on January 9, 1982, despite what this commemorative postal cancellation reads. The apparent discrepancy can be explained by the fact that the *Badger* left Ludington on the night of January 8th, but left Manitowoc on the return trip the morning of the 9th. (Author's collection.)

The *Spartan* was tied up at Ludington's No. 3 1/2 slip (shown here behind No. 3 slip) for many years after her lay-up in September 1979. She was steamed up in the spring of 1980 to run on a lease agreement with the Ann Arbor Railroad. However, plans were immediately scuttled when it was found that Frankfort, Michigan's harbor was too shallow for the deep-drafted *Spartan*. She has since been moved to No. 2 1/2 slip, where she remains today. (Photo by Steve Elve.)

Milwaukee's Daniel Hoan Memorial Harbor Bridge, opened in 1977, provided a dramatic entrance to the Jones Island car ferry slip. The slip was located to the left of the *Badger*, behind the paneled building. The ferry is shown outbound on a summer afternoon in 1980. (Photo by Art Chavez.)

The Harbor Bridge over Milwaukee's port entrance provided an excellent vantage point for photographing the car ferries. These ships ran continuously from this port from 1897 until the last freight trip on October 4, 1980. In this view, the *Badger* sports her Chessie sleeping cat silhouette in the letter "C" stack emblem. (Photo by Art Chavez.)

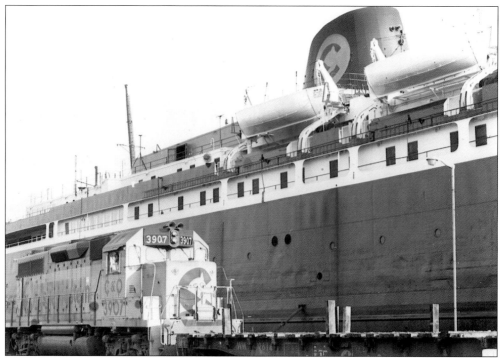

With two runs down and one to go, it appeared that Chessie would abandon its Kewaunee route in 1983. A group of Ludington business investors headed by hotel owner Glen Bowden worked behind the scenes. After working tirelessly to honor existing labor union contracts, they were successful in purchasing the railroad's three-ship operation on July 1, 1983. Chessie System's last load of freight is pushed aboard the City of Midland 41, with the *Badger* as a backdrop. (Photo by Robert Vande Vusse.)

The *Badger* moves into position at Ludington to take on her first load of passengers and autos for the newly formed Michigan-Wisconsin Transportation Company (M-WT). The transition from Chessie to M-WT ownership was smooth and orderly and the cost of the three car ferries was reported to have been $1. (Photo by Douglas S. Goodhue.)

Five

SERVICE HISTORY
MICHIGAN-WISCONSIN
TRANSPORTATION COMPANY

1983–1990

Michigan Wisconsin-Transportation Company's officers are, from left to right, Glen Bowden (president), William Bacon (superintendent of steamships), and George Towns (vice president). The men pose prior for their historic first trip aboard the *City of Midland 41* at Ludington on July 1, 1983. The car ferry route between Ludington and Kewaunee was classified as a shortline railroad. Chessie System signed a six-year agreement with M-WT to provide railroad switching service and routing of the new company's freight. The Midland handled freight, automobiles, and passengers year-round on the Kewaunee route; a week later the *Badger* was placed on a summer-only Ludington to Milwaukee run carrying exclusively automobiles and passengers. (Courtesy *Ludington Daily News*, photo by Todd Reed.)

One of M-WT's early advertisements was this 1983 flyer featuring the slogan "The Lake Michigan Connection." Fares were charged accordingly, as the Kewaunee run was four-hours in duration, and the Milwaukee run was six hours. Because of the one-year gap since the 1981 State of Michigan/Chessie run and the negative publicity during the railroad's abandonment efforts, many Milwaukee patrons were not aware of the reinstatement of service. (Author's collection.)

The *Badger* heads out of Milwaukee at 8 a.m. on a Sunday in July 1983. Due to the disappointingly low patronage, service to Milwaukee ended in 1984 after only two seasons. Part of the problem was M-WT's lack of money to mount an aggressive advertising campaign. The more successful Kewaunee run had no confusing gaps in service and enjoyed a large cross-country automobile trade, and due to the route's location up the lake, was a true short-cut. Milwaukee's proximity to Chicago gave travelers the option of driving around the bottom of the lake. (Photo by Douglas S. Goodhue.)

Capt. John Bissell was one of the C&O fleet's most affable skippers, always taking time out for passengers and ship enthusiasts alike. Standing atop the *Badger's* fanhouse in the middle of Lake Michigan are, from left to right, author Art Chavez, Doug Goodhue, John Bissell, and Tony Robles. The car ferry crews treated us like crew on dozens of trips, from our youth in the late 1970s to the present day. This photo was taken in August 1983. (Photo by Douglas S. Goodhue.)

The *Badger* is shown in her M-WT livery. The hull remained black and white, but Chessie's stack colors were retained until well into the 1983 season. The large disk was painted deep red at first, harking back to the Pere Marquette stack logo. Later, white interconnected lettering forming "MWT" was added, completing the simple design. (Photo by Art Chavez.)

This is a rear view of the *Badger* entering Kewaunee in her M-WT colors. At this point in her career, the ship was showing her age, particularly in the passenger areas. The lounge and stateroom furniture was faded and worn, and the overall appearance of her pastel-blue painted walls was becoming drab. However, scheduled service was still being maintained. (Photo by Art Chavez.)

The *Badger* was laid-up after the 1984 summer run to Milwaukee. The *City of Midland 41* exclusively provided M-WT's year-round Kewaunee service until 1988. The *Midland* was the ship of choice because of her 50-automobile capacity upper deck, leaving the main deck reserved for railcars. The *Badger's* upper deck could only accommodate 15 to 18 autos. The *Midland* is shown at Kewaunee with her upper deck in use. (Photo by Art Chavez)

The *City of Midland* ran until November 1988, when her coast guard certificate expired. M-WT faced the huge expense of renewing the ship's boiler mounts, which during annual inspection were found to be rotting away. Consequently, the *Badger* was brought back into service after four years of inactivity. The *Midland* is shown entering Kewaunee near the end of her career. (Photo by Art Chavez.)

This was one of M-WT's colorful 1985 ads featuring the *City of Midland 41*. It was the first year that the company ran a single ship, after dropping the Milwaukee route. The *Midland* provided excellent service until her retirement in 1988. (Author's collection.)

Brought out of mothballs in fall 1988, the *Badger* ran alone on the Ludington to Kewaunee run during M-WT's final years of service. During the summer months, passengers and automobiles were carried on the day trip, and railcars and a smaller number of people and autos were transported on the night sailing, particularly on the eastbound 2:30 a.m. trip out of Kewaunee. The *Badger* is shown here approaching Kewaunee harbor in 1989. (Photo by Art Chavez.)

Purser Ron Plowe walks up the *Badger's* steep gangplank, carrying a stack of schedules and the portable stateroom key rack. The purser is one of the last people to come aboard ship prior to departure. If they were fortunate, last minute stragglers were able to board via the freight loading apron and car deck, which at the time was normally off-limits to passengers. On rare occasion, if not far from the apron, the ship would turn back for late-arrivals. (Photo by Douglas S. Goodhue.)

A locomotive in Baltimore & Ohio Railroad livery pushes a heavy load of freight onto the *Badger's* car deck at Ludington. During its later years, M-WT had a freight contract that consisted of heavy tank cars loaded with liquefied clay. The cargo was unusually heavy and brought the ship's draft to the deepest point. In some situations, depending on Lake Michigan's water level, the ship would touch bottom (without damage) in Kewaunee harbor. (Photo by Dan Bissell.)

The *Badger* enters Kewaunee channel through a thin layer of broken ice near the end of the M-WT era. The ice problems that plagued the ferries in the 1960s and 1970s were non-existent in the later years, due to the mild winters. There were a few cold spells in the late 1980s, but the resulting ice was no comparison to that found in a sustained deep-freeze. (Photo by Art Chavez.)

Capt. Ernest G. Barth, right, watches the rudder indicator as his daughter LaVange and wheelsman Roger Vitucki focus on the *Badger's* gyrocompass repeater in an effort to keep the ship on course. This was Barth's retirement trip on September 29, 1989, marking the end of his 43-year career sailing on the Lake Michigan car ferries. (Photo by Douglas S. Goodhue.)

Glen Bowden announced that ferry service would be suspended indefinitely on Friday, November 16, 1990. Ostensibly, service was halted because the channel at Kewaunee needed dredging and the *Badger* was touching bottom. Bowden stated that if and when service was reinstated, it would be between Ludington and Manitowoc. The *Badger* is shown entering Kewaunee with her last westbound load of freight, which consisted of five loaded and three empty railcars. (Photo by Tom Younk.)

An impromptu sign is mounted on the nose of Green Bay & Western Railroad's Alco locomotive No. 312 after loading the final cargo of eastbound freight on November 16, 1990. Part of the ship's crew, the train crew, and enthusiasts pose for the electronic and print media covering the event. Nearly a century of cross-lake freight service to and from Kewaunee, which began on November 27, 1892, ended that day. (Photo by Tom Younk.)

Capt. Bruce Masse bids farewell to car ferry artist and historian Doug Goodhue on the *Badger's* final freight run. With Masse on the ship's cardeck and Goodhue on the dock, the two men symbolize the severance of service that began on nearly the same spot 98 years earlier. Minutes after this shot was taken, Masse took the *Badger* out of Kewaunee for the last time. M-WT filed for bankruptcy protection later that winter. (Photo by Ken Ottmann.)

Six

SERVICE HISTORY
LAKE MICHIGAN
CARFERRY SERVICE

1992–PRESENT

Charles Conrad, shown here in 1936 as assistant purser on the Pere Marquette car ferry *City of Saginaw 31*, inherited a life-long love of the car ferries from his father, Chief Engineer James Conrad, of the same ship. Little did young Charles know that five decades after this photo was taken, he would have the financial means to save the car ferries for the people of Ludington after M-WT filed for bankruptcy. He ensured that a new generation of travelers would have the opportunity to appreciate the convenience and importance of the cross-lake ferry service. (Courtesy Sharla Manglitz.)

After nearly a year of legal battles with the courts and M-WT's creditors, Lake Michigan Carferry Service (LMC) succeeded in its attempt at resuming cross-lake service. Charles Conrad invested his own money to refurbish the *Badger* to cater to the passenger and automobile trade. M-WT would go on record as the last Lake Michigan railroad ferry operator. The *Badger* is shown leaving Ludington in LMC stack livery. (Photo by Ken Ottmann.)

Charles Conrad, who gained business success from the climate-control equipment firm he founded, was honored for his altruistic move of investing his own resources to maintain the historic car ferry link between Michigan and Wisconsin. He was honored in both states for his tireless efforts and ultimate success in revitalizing a new "passenger-friendly" service. Conrad is shown accepting an award from the Michigan Historic Preservation Network in 1993. (Courtesy Conrad family, photo by Bruce A. Nelson.)

LMC resumed ferry service on May 16, 1992, between Ludington and Manitowoc. The firm's management team, consisting of Charles Conrad, Don Clingan, and Jim Anderson, concluded that Manitowoc was the most promising Wisconsin port. Their decision proved valid, as 100,000 passengers and 30,000 autos were carried during the inaugural season. The *Badger* is shown arriving at Chicago in 1995, greeted by a water cannon salute. (Photo by Art Chavez.)

Charles Conrad died on February 9, 1995. His son-in-law, Robert Manglitz, had assumed the role of LMC's president in 1993. Before his death, Conrad was assured of the *Badger's* success with a solid group of ship and shore-based personnel and a hands-on management team. The annual patronage figures were increasing and the service received high remarks from passengers. The *Badger* is shown approaching Chicago's nearly finished Navy Pier tourist attraction. (Photo by Art Chavez.)

The *Badger* arrived at Navy Pier on May 15, 1995. She was dubbed the "Michigan Vacation Showboat" and was used as a floating exhibition hall showcasing Michigan's tourism industry. The ship's car deck was covered with red carpeting and exhibitor's booths were set up. Among the vendors were the Henry Ford Museum of Dearborn and the Grand Hotel of Mackinac Island. The *Badger* was moored at the pier for three days. (Photo by Art Chavez.)

Many Ludington-area residents took advantage of the *Badger's* three-day visit to Chicago. Passengers traveled for $115 round trip, which took about eight hours each way. People had the option to stay aboard ship in the staterooms, but were also offered special room rates in downtown Chicago. The event was cosponsored by the Michigan Travel Bureau and the *Chicago Tribune*. (Photo by Art Chavez.)

Merchant vessels are required by US Coast Guard and American Bureau of Shipping regulations to undergo a hull inspection every five years. At times a ship is required to enter drydock unscheduled to undergo emergency hull repairs. This view shows the *Badger* in the graving dock at Bay Shipbuilding at Sturgeon Bay, Wisconsin. (Photo by Art Chavez.)

The *Badger* is shown back at her Sturgeon Bay birthplace. Part of Bay Shipbuilding Company's sprawling yard is located on the former Christy Corporation property. This view shows the sharp flare of the *Badger's* icebreaking bow and her broad, square hull, and relatively shallow draft. Note how small her starboard propeller is in relation to the ship's mass. (Photo by Art Chavez.)

The steamer *Pere Marquette* of 1897 pioneered the twin screw configuration and hull-enclosed, ice-protected propeller shafts of the Lake Michigan car ferries. Most of the ships in the late 19th and early 20th century had exposed shafts and support brackets. Naval architect Robert Logan recognized this weakness, and the *Badger* still carries his innovative design while resting on her keel blocks in this photo. (Photo by Art Chavez.)

This photo, taken c. 1993, looks north at Ludington from the rusting hulk of the former Ann Arbor car ferry *Arthur K. Atkinson*. The *Badger* loads autos in No. 2 slip, and her sistership, *Spartan*, lies tied alongside the *Atkinson* at No. 2 1/2 slip. (Photo by Art Chavez.)

Capt. Gregg Andersen stands at the *Badger's* engine order telegraphs as he takes his ship out of Ludington in September of 1994. At the time of his appointment, he was one of the youngest skippers on the Great Lakes. During the winter months in lay-up, Andersen stripped the paint off and restored most of the brass hardware in the *Badger's* pilothouse, and hand-built the ship's wooden navigational instrument console. (Photo by Art Chavez.)

The *Badger* heads into a Lake Michigan swell on a windy fall day in 1994. The empty bow deck is quite a contrast to the midsummer crowds that usually sunned themselves on the lounge chairs, now stacked and secured, visible in the foreground. LMC's operating season runs from mid-May through mid-October. This view was taken from the ship's port bridgewing. (Photo by Art Chavez.)

On an early summer morning, the *Badger* takes on a load of autos at Ludington. The glassed-in area on the aft upper deck is a wood-planked lounge that was added after LMC refurbished the ship. The gangplank is no longer used for the embarkation of passengers; large stairways, which include a wheelchair lift, provide access on the car deck. (Photo by Max Hanley.)

This view looks aft on the *Badger's* former railroad car deck in 1994. Now paved with asphalt, the vehicles no longer risk damaging their tires on the railroad tracks. In 1996, a mid-deck was added to either side of the outer edges of the car deck to accommodate additional vehicles. The inside lanes were left unobstructed for high-sided semis, motor homes, and busses. (Photo by Art Chavez.)

When they appeared in the 1950s, the *Badger* and *Spartan's* full-width pilothouses were a design feature that set them apart from other Great Lakes car ferries. The pilothouses provided the navigation crew with protection from the weather, and allowed them near-360-degree visibility through the 25 large windows that surrounded the bridge. (Photo by Art Chavez.)

A happy couple poses in front of the *Badger's* bronze builder's plate, below the pilothouse. This is a popular spot for photographers to frame their subjects. Other popular areas for photo shoots include the lifeboats and life-ring stations. (Photo by Max Hanley.)

Capt. Bruce Masse, left, and Capt. Dean Hobbs are among several skippers that have been employed by Lake Michigan Carferry Service. They include Masse (now retired), Hobbs (currently senior captain), Kevin Fitch (current captain), Gregg Andersen, and Larry Riker. Because of the 24-hour, seven-day-a-week nature of the summer peak season of service, two captains alternate on a two-days-on, two-days-off schedule. (Photo by Max Hanley.)

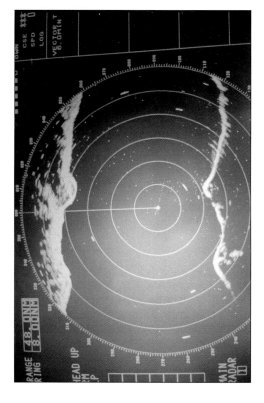

This image is from the *Badger's* main radar unit, a Furuno model FR 2830 S. The maximum 48-mile range setting is in place, and the outline of Lake Michigan's mid-section is clearly visible. The *Badger* is westbound near the center of the lake, with the beam from the center point (representing the ship) projecting along the course toward Manitowoc. Each concentric ring represents an area of 8 nautical miles. (Photo by Art Chavez.)

"We launch great vacations!"

The fun you'll have sailing on the S.S. Badger is certain to bring a smile to your face long after you've returned home. Your family will reminisce about the magic of cruising aboard a 410-foot ship, the majesty of Lake Michigan, and the feeling that you've experienced a truly special vacation. The four-hour cruise between Michigan and Wisconsin is just long enough to enjoy dining aboard the ship, live entertainment, and free Badger Bingo. Daily sailings mid-May through mid-October. Senior discounts and travel packages available.

LAKE MICHIGAN CARFERRY
800-841-4243

BADGER

MANITOWOC ● ● LUDINGTON

As this full-page magazine advertisement proclaims, Lake Michigan Carferry Service is in the "people" business. For many, the *Badger* is not just a means of transport, but a destination in her own right. LMC has succeeded in making the crossing a memorable experience that brings people back year after year. Capt. Bruce Masse is shown in the inset. (Author's collection.)

The *Badger* arrives at Ludington on a warm summer evening. LMC periodically runs 2-hour cruises along the shorelines off Ludington and Manitowoc. The ship is also used for proms by area high schools. (Photo by Max Hanley.)

A full service gift shop was created when LMC refurbished the *Badger*. C&O and M-WT never took the time nor spent the money to make the ship into an attractive tourist-oriented experience. The C&O lacked the interest, and M-WT had neither the capital nor the savvy to do a credible makeover. (Photo by Max Hanley.)

Every summer, a variety of groups and organizations use the *Badger* to get to regional and national conventions. Among these are Harley-Davidson and Triumph motorcycle groups, steam engine enthusiasts, and many different auto clubs. Here, a group of Ford Model A owners drive aboard the *Badger* to attend a convention in Wisconsin. (Photo by Max Hanley.)

A group of party-goers enjoy themselves in the *Badger's* lounge during a shoreline cruise. These are usually held a few times each year in the spring and early summer, during the off-peak season. The cruises are often based on a theme, such as a 1950s sock hop or in a Hawaiian or Caribbean style. (Photo by Max Hanley.)

The *Badger's* maritime museum gallery doubles as the site of children's entertainment programs. College students who comprise the ship's entertainment staff conduct coloring contests, magic demonstrations, and puppet shows. There are also "Badger Bingo" sessions held in the main lounge, as well as karaoke. (Photo by Max Hanley.)

Groups of car ferry and Great Lakes shipping enthusiasts meet aboard the *Badger* for formal and informal get-togethers every summer. The ship also has quite a following among those interested in steam propulsion. Pictured from left to right are JoLynn Hanley, Mike Modderman, Roxy Wienand, Jean Wienand, and Julie Schnoor. (Photo by Max Hanley.)

Max Hanley, LMC's official photographer, captured this image of the *Badger* from Ludington's north breakwall. The north breakwater lighthouse was activated in 1924, and since then has guided the car ferries into port at the completion of countless Lake Michigan voyages. (Photo by Max Hanley.)

With her seagate opening up, the *Badger* heads into Ludington's channel after a trip from Manitowoc. The coast guard can be seen on security detail escorting the ferry into port. All merchant vessels are escorted inbound and outbound by port security. (Photo by Max Hanley.)

The *Badger* is shown entering Ludington's channel after a rough crossing on Lake Michigan. In such instances, the ship's course is altered to head the bow into the high seas as much as possible. This helps to minimize the ship's rolling motion, and does much for the comfort of the passengers. (Photo by Roxy Wienand.)

During the off-season, the *Badger* undergoes mechanical and cosmetic maintenance work and governmental safety and health inspections. One of the rituals of spring, prior to each new season of operation, is the lighting of the ship's boilers. Max Hanley is shown hunched over with a torch, about to light the kindling inside one of the fireboxes in the starboard-side, forward boiler. (Photo by JoLynn Hanley.)

The *Badger's* cardeck has undergone two major alterations over the years. In 1964, the overhead clearance was increased by 18 inches to accommodate taller railcars. In 1996, a mid-deck was added (visible in this photo) to handle over 40 additional automobiles. Here, the ship's portside car deck is filled with Harley-Davidsons, enroute to the motorcycle firm's 95th anniversary celebration in Milwaukee in June 1998. (Photo by Andy Rose.)

The *Badger* has three engine room work shifts, called watches, working 4 hours on and 8 hours off in a 24-hour period. This particular watch includes, from left to right, Mike Root, Jeff Usiak, Andy Rose, Randy Robotham, Bob Reams, and Eric Roberts. (Photo by Max Hanley.)

Inside the *Badger's* port engine, seated around one of the crossheads of a connecting rod are, from left to right, Randy Robotham, Mike Braybrook, Lonnie Anderson, and Senior Chief Engineer Charles Cart. The engine was thoroughly overhauled after the 2001 sailing season. The starboard engine gets similar treatment after the 2002 season. Even though the steam engines are 50 years old and require high levels of maintenance, they have proven to be efficient and very reliable. (Photo by Max Hanley.)

This view shows the unique configuration of a Skinner Engine Company steeple piston assembly. Two pistons (high pressure on top, and low pressure on the bottom) are arranged on a single piston rod in a "steeple" formation. Usually a rod has a single piston arrangement. For additional details, refer to Appendix D. (Photo by Max Hanley.)

The *Badger's* engines and boilers were designated as a "Historical Mechanical Engineering Landmark" by the American Society of Mechanical Engineers in 1996. Recognizing this historically significant element to their operation, LMC strives to maintain the ship's propulsion system, despite its age and the occasional challenges it creates for the engineering staff. (Photo by Max Hanley.)

Lake Michigan is one of the only places on earth where one can still ride a large coal-burning steamship. With the skill and dedication of her crew, the *Badger* will offer this opportunity for many years to come. (Photo by Max Hanley.)

At the beginning of the 2003 sailing season, the *Badger* celebrated her 50th anniversary. She is shown being moored at Ludington's Waterfront Park on May 15th in preparation for a rechristening ceremony. Swinging the bottle of champagne was Sharla Manglitz, granddaughter of LMC's founder Charles Conrad. She was accompanied on the stand by her mother Janet Manglitz and grandmother Elsie Conrad. The ship later departed on an afternoon shoreline cruise for invited guests, media and dignitaries, kicking off Michigan Week tourism and history-related celebrations. (Photo by Art Chavez.)

The *Badger* frequently partners with groups and organizations to promote regional interest in attractions around Ludington, West Michigan, Manitowoc, Door County and beyond. This is part of the program distributed during the 2003 rechristening. (Art Chavez Collection.)

Seven

THE LEGACY CONTINUES
2003 AND BEYOND

The celebratory year of 2003 also brought uncertainty to the Ludington ferry operation with the announcement of a new start-up competitor car ferry operation 50 miles south in Muskegon. *Lake Express* stated that a new 192-foot aluminum hulled high-speed catamaran car ferry was under construction by Austal shipbuilding in Mobile, Alabama. *Lake Express* was resurrecting the *Milwaukee Clipper* route to Milwaukee, which ceased operation in 1970. The new vessel could cross Lake Michigan at 40 mph in 2.5 hours and could carry 46 automobiles and 250 passengers. Ludington officials expressed concern there was not enough business to support two ferry routes. The *Lake Express* ferry debuted in 2004, and history has proven that the *Badger* and *Lake Express* cater to different markets. (Photo by Art Chavez.)

Over the years, the *Badger* has received numerous awards of distinction and commendation, including the Ship of the Year Award by the Steamship Historical Society of America in 2002. In 2009, she was placed on the National Register of Historic Places by the Department of the Interior. (Photo by Douglas S. Goodhue.)

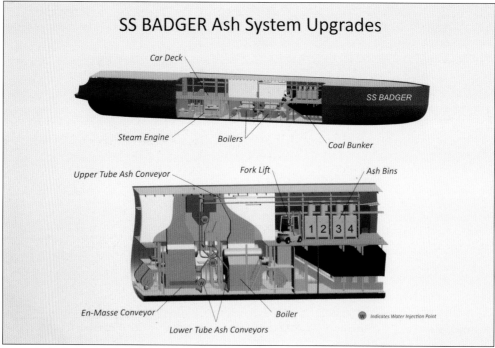

In 2011, the *Badger*'s owners began a lengthy correspondence with the US Environmental Protection Agency to conform to new standards eliminating the discharge of coal ash into the lake from the ship's boilers. The process was politically charged and is well documented. New boiler combustion controls and an ash retention system were installed at a cost of $2.4 million. LMC had been continually improving and upgrading the efficiency of the *Badger*'s boilers and engines since it assumed ownership in 1992. (Photo by Douglas S. Goodhue.)

The *Badger*'s ash retention system was operational at the start of the 2015 sailing season. The complex system was a challenge for both LMC engineers and those from Hapman, manufacturer of the tubular chain-drag conveyor system that was installed to transfer coal ash from beneath the ship's boilers to storage bins on the car deck. The ash is recycled for use in cement production. Project manager Joe Zerbel stated that it "combined the expert application and design of Hapman conveyors with an unrelenting, ambitious and capable customer" in LMC staff. "When both teams step up with a resourceful, collaborative spirit, viable solutions can be found for 'impossible' material handling challenges." (Photo by Stephanie Parkinson.)

On the weekend of April 14–15, 2018, a strong spring storm brought high northeasterly winds reaching 50 mph and tremendous waves onto the west shore of Lake Michigan. The Manitowoc car ferry dock structure and asphalt roadway sustained extensive erosion damage as the outer breakwater was ineffective at holding back the force of the heavy waves. The damage struck at a bad time, as the *Badger*'s sailing season was slated to begin in less than a month, on May 11. Earlier, in 2016, Foth, an infrastructure and environmental engineering services firm, was hired to conduct long-term plans to improve the *Badger*'s dock facilities in Ludington and Manitowoc. (Courtesy WBAY.)

Immediate engineering work to assess the damage was initiated by Foth, and the City of Manitowoc, owner of the dock, applied for an emergency repair grant from the State of Wisconsin. On May 1, the governor's office announced the award of $800,000 from the state's Harbor Assistance Program to fund the repairs. Work was carried out by Manitowoc's McMullen & Pitz Construction Company. The marine contracting and engineering firm was established in 1918 and has a reputation for high quality work. McMullen & Pitz has extensive experience over the last century at building and maintaining car ferry docks on both sides of Lake Michigan. Their involvement assured that *Badger*'s dock would be ready for the 2018 season. (Courtesy WBAY.)

At the end of the *Badger*'s 2018 sailing season in October, extensive overall upgrades to the dock facilities at both Ludington and Manitowoc began. A 420-foot timber fender system and sheet pile dock wall was constructed at Manitowoc, with physical work carried out by McMullen & Pitz. The overall project was headed by Foth. A 260-foot timber fender wall system was also installed at Ludington. The old ferry slips, constructed new in the 1930s, were continually renewed in small segments as needed due to wear and tear of usage and the ravages of time and weather. These took their toll on the structures and eventually the old pilings and fender structures needed replacement. (Photo by Ken Ottmann.)

Funding for the dock improvements was made possible by a $5 million US Department of Transportation grant from FASTLANE (Fostering Advancements in Shipping and Transportation for the Long-Term Achievement of National Efficiencies). This was in addition to a $4 million grant from the State of Wisconsin Department of Transportation's HAP (Harbor Assistance Program) fund. Of the HAP funding, $1 million was allocated previously to the emergency repairs for the Manitowoc storm damage. (Photo by Ken Ottmann.)

The *Badger*'s cavernous car deck was built to carry railroad cars, so when LMC was asked to haul extremely long wind turbine parts, it was not a problem. The tractor/trailers hauling them saved time, fuel, and costly permits to allow the oversized loads to pass through multiple jurisdictions in Wisconsin, Illinois, Indiana, and Michigan. (Courtesy Lake Michigan Carferry.)

The officers and crew of the car ferry operation have always been friendly and pleased to meet passengers interested in the ship and its history. Here, Capt. Jeffery Curtis meets longtime car ferry enthusiast Stephanie Parkinson in the *Badger*'s aft pilothouse. Stephanie's father, Timothy Parkinson, was a locomotive engineer for the Chessie System/CSX Railroad. He worked the Grand Rapids, Ludington and Manistee subdivisions. (Photo by Lisa Parkinson.)

Sr. Capt. Michael Martin has worked 26 years aboard the *Badger*, 9 of them as captain. He has a great appreciation for the ship's history and what it means to the communities along the lakeshore, and to the passengers that sail aboard with him. He learned his boat handling skills by working with Capt. Bruce Masse and Capt. Dean Hobbs. (Photo by Shelby Soberalski)

In 2015, the *Badger* was designated a continuation of US Highway 10. The route currently stretches westward from Bay City, Michigan, to Fargo, North Dakota. Originally established in 1926, stretching from Detroit to Seattle, the interstate highway system has diminished the length of this route considerably. For a time, the designation was painted on the ship's sea gate. (Photo by Trevor Aaron Suarez.)

With John Brandt looking on, wheelsman Jeff Dodge instructs Lydia Chavez on the art of steering a 410-foot steamboat across Lake Michigan. The 60-mile route between Manitowoc and Ludington saw the lake's first steel railroad car ferry established there in 1897. The *Badger* is the last of that type of ship built, in 1953. (Photo by Kristin Ottmann Nesbit.)

On a beautiful spring evening, May 19, 2021, the brightly lit *Badger* awaits her inaugural sailing the next morning from Ludington to Manitowoc under the ownership of Interlake Maritime Services. The fair weather continued for the season's first voyage, much to the delight of passengers and dignitaries who were aboard. (Photo by Ken Ottmann.)

The *Badger*'s annual maiden voyage brings friends together for the opening of the summer sailing season each May. From left to right are Audrey Robertson Boals (daughter of Bernard Robertson, the *Badger*'s first captain), Ken Ottmann, Linda Spencer, Kristin Ottmann Nesbit, Tim Foster, Trish Ottmann, and Tom Read. (Courtesy Kristin Ottmann Nesbit.)

The *Badger* enters the basin inside Manitowoc's breakwater as she prepares to make her turn and drop anchor on approach to her slip. Car ferries never required assistance from tugboats in docking. Their own powerful twin propellers were used to maneuver the ships in tight quarters. (Photo by Trevor Aaron Suarez.)

The *Badger* flies the house flag of her new owners, Interlake Steamship Co., while finishing backing into her slip on May 20, 2021. The City of Manitowoc enthusiastically welcomes the *Badger* on her first trip every spring, with schoolchildren holding welcome signs and greetings by the mayor and other city officials. (Photo by Trevor Aaron Suarez.)

This view clearly shows the new fender wall structure in the *Badger*'s ferry slip. It utilizes timber facing and sheet pile backing with rubber cushions sandwiched in between. The ship's forward lines are shown being winched taut during docking. (Photo by Trevor Aaron Suarez.)

The *Badger* turns eastbound out of her Manitowoc slip and heads for the breakwater gap and open water for her four-hour journey to Ludington. Connor Siemers, left, and Brock Johnson take photographs and are the latest generation of young enthusiasts who take an interest in Great Lakes maritime history. (Photo by Douglas S. Goodhue.)

The *Badger* is shown backing into her slip after returning from a two-hour evening shoreline cruise along the Wisconsin shore in 2022. Lake Michigan Carferry hosts these themed day and evening cruises several times a season from both Ludington and Manitowoc. (Photo by Douglas S. Goodhue.)

Disembarking her shoreline cruise passengers at Manitowoc, the *Badger* awaits a load of automobiles and passengers for the return trip home to Ludington in July 2022. (Photo by Trevor Aaron Suarez.)

The beauty of a summer Lake Michigan sunset is something to be experienced aboard the *Badger*. Ken and Trish Ottmann enjoy a shoreline cruise on July 30, 2022. The theme was Through the Decades, and the event featured live music and food. (Photo by Kristin Ottmann Nesbit.)

Leaving Manitowoc with a setting August sun in her wake, the *Badger* carries a full load of happy shoreline passengers as she steams out into Lake Michigan. Passengers typically board the Wisconsin evening cruises at 7:30 p.m. with departure at 8:00 p.m. and return at 10:00 p.m. Michigan departures were an hour later, eastern standard time. (Photo by Trevor Aaron Suarez.)

Eight

LOOKING BACK AT THE *BADGER* AFTER SEVEN DECADES

The *Spartan*, lead ship in the two-vessel class and twin sister of the *Badger*, is shown with colorful flags flying in Ludington's No. 2 slip. She has just arrived on her maiden voyage on Thursday, October 23, 1952, after a trip from Milwaukee. She had been on public exhibition there and carried no freight, as the C&O fleet was in the midst of a 114-day work stoppage. Two days after the *Spartan*'s arrival, the Great Lakes Licensed Officers Organization settled the labor strike. The new ship's arrival and public festivities welcoming her are credited with bringing both sides of the dispute to accord. (Photo by Ted Schultz, Steve Elve Collection.)

The *Spartan*, shown with the strike-idled *City of Midland 41* and *Pere Marquette 18*, was the first Ludington ferry to carry the railroad's "C and O For Progress" stack herald. Chesapeake & Ohio Railway's first iteration of the stack herald came in 1950. It was two interconnected "C" and "O" letters, without the "For Progress." The 1950 "C" and "O" letters were five feet high, and the word "and" was eight inches high. The 1952 "C" and "O" letters were four feet six inches high. The words "and" and "for" were six inches high, with "Progress" at nine inches high. The C&O fleet's original stack color was dark blue, called "Enchantment Blue," as were the letters. The twelve-foot diameter disc found on the modern, single-stack ships in the fleet was "Federal Yellow." (Photo by Ted Schultz, Steve Elve Collection.)

On March 16, 1953, the *Badger* was fitted to Kewaunee's south apron at No. 1 slip for track adjustment and where she took on her first load of coal cars for fuel. The *Spartan* had arrived earlier for a load before the *Badger* arrived from the shipyard. Later, the pair went out in the lake eastbound for a time to cruise together for publicity photos. The *Spartan* is shown with a bone in her teeth just before the *Badger* heads north to Christy Corporation's yard in Sturgeon Bay for final adjustments and fit-out. (Photo by Ted Schultz, Steve Elve Collection.)

The *Badger*'s maiden voyage took place from Manitowoc on March 21, 1953. All three Wisconsin ports participated in their own "maiden voyage" cargoes in the ensuing days. Area manufacturers proudly shipped entire train loads of tractors, automobiles, and paper. Here, Green Bay & Western's Alco switch engine pushes a load of Green Bay paper across the *Badger*'s loading apron at Kewaunee. (Photo by Ted Schultz, Steve Elve Collection.)

With the *Badger*'s pilothouse momentarily cleared of dignitaries, the wheelsman adjusts the magnifier on the gyrocompass repeater as the mate on watch takes bearings on the newly installed radio direction finder. (Photo by Ted Schultz, Steve Elve Collection.)

The wheelsman keeps on course in the *Badger*'s pilothouse. The equipment, from left to right, are the wheelsman's telegraph, to receive order from the captain in the aft pilothouse to place rudder amidships while docking; steering wheel and gyrocompass repeater; magnetic compass binnacle; Raytheon radar unit; whistle pulls in the event of engine order telegraph malfunction; and engine order telegraphs, also known as "Chadburns." (Photo by Ted Schultz, Steve Elve Collection.)

On Sunday March 22, 1953, the C&O Railway hosted a public exhibition aboard the *Badger* in No. 2 slip at Ludington. Public interest and support of Chesapeake & Ohio's car ferries was at a high point in the mid-1950s. The ferry operation and connecting railyards was a major employer and used numerous Ludington businesses to support the fleet with bakery, laundry, and hardware services, to name a few. The large number of cars in the parking lot during the exhibition shows that civic enthusiasm. (Photo by Ted Schultz, Steve Elve Collection)

A floral arrangement in the *Badger*'s passenger lounge is representative of the ship's namesake, the University of Wisconsin Badgers athletic team, and its colors of red and white. (Photo by Ted Schultz, Steve Elve Collection.)

The *Badger* awaits thousands of visitors during her day-long open house. The ship's original colors were a departure from earlier ferries in the fleet. Her top band along the boat deck was white, followed by a gray band that looks black in many photos (see page 52, bottom photo). The cabin deck was highlighted by a wide white band above the black painted hull. The stack was dark blue with a yellow disc, and dark blue lettering of the company herald. The fan house beneath the stack was a medium gray. The radar, forward and aft masts, and fittings atop the pilothouse were painted dark blue. (Photo by Ted Schultz, Steve Elve Collection.)

Immediately aft on the cabin deck was the aft pilothouse and an open area for passengers to lounge in the sun. At the top of the stairway leading up to the next level, the boat deck, was an open-air seating area. This was to serve as outdoor seating for the dining room. It was intended to be covered by a canvas awning to protect passengers from coal soot. The awning's framework is visible in this photo, but was seldom used. This area would be covered over in 1960 as extra automobile space. (Photo by Ted Schultz, Steve Elve Collection.)

The *Badger*'s pilothouse is filled with excited visitors as they tour the new ship. Most areas were open to the public, with the possible exception of the engine and boiler rooms, due to the cramped spaces and heavy machinery. Private tours in smaller groups were accommodated below decks. (Photo by Ted Schultz, Steve Elve Collection.)

A mishap occurred on the *Badger*'s loading apron at No. 2 slip in Ludington. More than likely, a railcar was pushed too hard forward by the switch crew, ramming the car against the bumping post in the bow section of the car deck. This pushed the ship away from the apron, causing it to drop, and damaging the right side counterweight. The ship sustained no damage, other than some prematurely scuffed paint. (Photo by Ted Schultz, Steve Elve Collection.)

It's freight business as usual, which was the primary reason for the *Badger*'s early existence. She is shown leaning heavily on her portside as a load of cars is pushed aboard at Maple Street slip in Milwaukee. This view from around 1955 shows the top gray band in the process of being painted black. (Photo by Jim Gregorski.)

During the 1960s, the C&O Railway began carrying trailers on flatcars. In corporate documents and reports, they were referred by the acronym TOFC. Informally, they were called piggybacks. This form of intermodal transport was gaining popularity and was the forerunner to modern sea containers shipping on specialized flatcars. This view is on the *Badger*'s aft port car deck. The light load uses only the center tracks, with automobiles taking up space alongside. (Photo by Jim Gregorski.)

The weather is apparently fair in this view forward on the *Badger*'s starboard car deck. The flatcars are secured by only a screw jack at each corner to keep the load from rocking. If heavy weather was predicted, additional chains would be used. If the weather was particularly severe, the piggybacks would be held back awaiting calmer seas. (Photo by Jim Gregorski.)

This 1970 view from the *Badger*'s bow looks east as she departs No. 3 slip and passes the *Pere Marquette 21*, moored alongside the *Spartan*. Both are laid up for inspection. Ludington's No. 3 slip was generally used by Milwaukee-bound boats, No. 2 slip for the Manitowoc run, and No. 1 slip for bound for Kewaunee and Manitowoc-Soo Line slip. (Photo by Jim Gregorski.)

The Pullman-style blankets found aboard passenger trains hint at Chesapeake & Ohio's railroad heritage that carried over to its car ferry fleet. The blankets sport the "C and O For Progress" design—the most distinctive herald in the railroad's long history. The *Badger* and *Spartan* had 60 passenger staterooms, 44 of them facing outward with a window, toilet, sink, and two beds. One converted from a couch, and the other folded down from the wall. The 16 inside rooms lacked a window but were slightly larger and had a shower. (Photo by John Hausmann.)

This view looks forward in the passenger lounge and down the portside stateroom hallway. The even-numbered rooms were located here. On the left is the snack bar that sold hot sandwiches, popcorn, potato chips, and the iconic Beer That Made Milwaukee Famous. (Photo by John Hausmann.)

This vantage point looks across mid-lounge toward the starboard side. Fleet upholsterer Bob Nash stated that all of the ferries had at least one extra piece of each style of furniture in the marine shop adjacent to No. 3 slip. The pieces would be unbolted from their floor anchors and switched out with a newly repaired or completely reupholstered chair or settee. The upholstery fabric was heavy and durable, with each furniture piece requiring reupholstering every ten years or so. Furniture on some ships like the *City of Midland* that came out with leather furniture covering would eventually be replaced with Naugahyde for ease of maintenance. (Photo by John Hausmann.)

This view shows clearly the design of the knock-off Eero Saarinen "Womb Chairs" and "Womb Settees." These pieces by Martin-Parry were covered with a heavy rubberized fabric and were more rugged than the more elegantly upholstered original Womb Chair manufactured by Knoll. Both designs shared the same sleek mid-century modern aesthetic. A distinguishing difference is Martin-Parry's heavier tubular steel frame and legs that have a geometry better suited for the rigors of shipboard service. (Photo by John Hausmann.)

The *Spartan*'s dining room still retains the refinement of C&O's passenger train dining service in this 1970 view. Gone are the linen napkins, replaced with an attractive heavy paper napkin adorned with the Chessie kitten. Placemats with blueprint drawings of the ship added to the rail/marine ambiance. (Photo by John Hausmann.)

This scene from 1956 was taken from the passenger liner/auto ferry *Aquarama*. The *Spartan* awaits departure from Milwaukee's Jones Island ferry slip. Passengers were treated to the aroma of the sprawling municipal sewage treatment plant located adjacent to the slip. Hot summer days were memorable in more ways than just a pleasant lake crossing. (Photo by Jim Gregorski.)

This classic view from the *Spartan*'s bow shows the enclosed, cantilevered bridge wings that were unique to her and the *Badger* in the lake ferry fleet. The original lattice radar antenna installed on the ship in 1952 was replaced with a bar-type unit in 1977. A distinguishing feature between the *Spartan* and *Badger* are the lights below the pilothouse windows. The *Badger* lacks this detail. (Photo by John Hausmann.)

The *Spartan*'s car deck tracks were referred to, from left to right, as Port Wing, Port Center, Starboard Center, and Starboard Wing. The heaviest and longest railcars were placed on the center tracks. Longer cars had difficulty making the curve on the wing tracks on the ship's stern. (Photo by John Hausmann.)

The *Spartan* takes on freight at the old No. 1 slip at Ludington in November 1977. It had not been used in several years, with the fleet downsizing from six to three ships. No. 3 slip's pilings had fallen into disrepair, prompting Chessie System to use in 1976 the old, weakened slip No. 1. It was short-lived, as in December 1977 the apron collapsed while the *Badger* was being loaded. The apron was severely damaged when a tank car dropped into the lake in 25 feet of water. The structure was never used again and was eventually dismantled. (Photo by Gregg Andersen.)

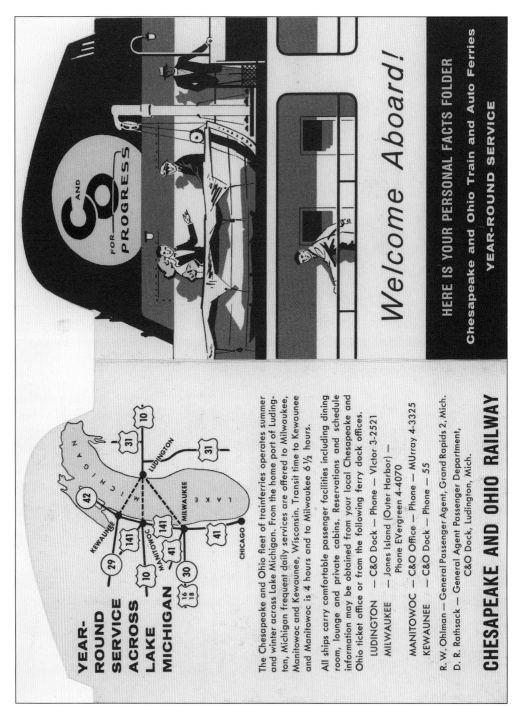

This is a promotional folder distributed aboard Chesapeake & Ohio Railway's car ferries beginning in 1954. (Author's collection.)

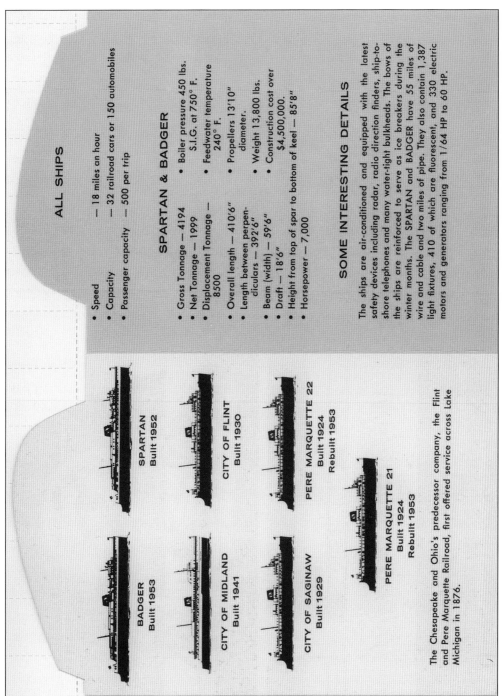

There were two additional versions of this folder. One depicted the stack lettering reversed to yellow lettering and a solid blue stack, circa 1961. The other listed six ships instead of seven, after the *City of Flint* was sold in 1969. (Author's collection.)

This is a cutaway view of the *Badger* as she looked in Lake Michigan Carferry colors. (Author's collection.)

137

Appendix A

REMEMBERING THE BADGER'S FIRST SKIPPER, CAPT. BERNARD "BUNNY" ROBERTSON
by Art Chavez

He greeted me at the front door of his Ludington home early one afternoon in May 1991. The old man's thin, spry frame was topped off by a white crew-cut hairstyle. His now bespectacled 84-year-old eyes were alert—much the same way they surely were while he was in command of the car ferry *Badger*, when he brought her out new from the Christy Corporation shipyard at Sturgeon Bay, Wisconsin, some 38 years earlier. I was about to interview Capt. Bernard A. "Bunny" Robertson, who had followed in the footsteps of his father, legendary Pere Marquette car ferry skipper Capt. Charles E. Robertson.

Back in 1990 when I first began conducting oral history interviews with people involved with the Ludington car ferries, I spoke to many colorful individuals. Perhaps my biggest thrill was getting to know Bunny Robertson. Surprisingly, he was initially reluctant to be interviewed. He humbly explained to me by telephone that he had an unremarkable career, and that he would be a boring interview. I knew little about him, other than that he brought out the *Badger* in 1953 and retired as her master in 1969. Fortunately, I had done a great deal of research into the early Pere Marquette ferry operations. This allowed me to rattle off dates and locations of major incidents and the names of many long-forgotten captains and crew. After conversing about 15 minutes, Bunny relented by saying, "You know, I haven't thought of some of those people you mentioned in 50 years! What did you say your name was? Come on over at tomorrow at 1:00 p.m."

As he closed the door, Captain Robertson motioned for me to have a seat in his living room. I was well prepared—armed with an audio-tape recorder and pages of notes with insightful questions to ask of him. I felt a bit nervous, as I was hoping not to tire the man out with a long-winded session, yet still be able get interesting answers that would lead to a rewarding interview. My concern was brief, as we warmed up to each other almost immediately. We spent about three hours chatting during that first visit. He clearly enjoyed it as much as I did, with both of us laughing at many of his old memories. His eyes sparkled as he told me of one adventure after another. I learned of Bunny's early days on the car ferries, before the advent of radar and modern navigation devices. He described in detail how in foggy conditions water depth was ascertained by throwing out the "sounding lead," a coiled rope marked at various depths by knots, rags, and strips of leather, with a lead weight tied at the bottom. There was also a harrowing account of attempts to re-secure rolling railcars that had broken loose during a storm. Captain Robertson's memory and sharp wit was impressive. At the first sign of his tiring, I brought our conversation to a close. We both enjoyed the time and made arrangements for another visit three weeks later. I was elated as I walked out to my car and knew that I was capturing a great deal of car ferry history that would otherwise be lost forever. During my drive home to Milwaukee, I listened to those tapes and began mentally preparing a new set of questions for our next meeting.

On my subsequent visits to Ludington, I usually recorded my interviews. But there were times I was in town on other research, when I would stop in to say hello and chat informally without prepared notes or a tape recorder. Bunny proudly told me that his father Charles had brought out new three PM car ferries from the yard at Manitowoc Shipbuilding Co.: the *Pere Marquette 21* in 1924, the *City of Saginaw 31* in 1929, and the *City of Midland 41* in 1941. I also learned that the old car ferries in the early 1920s regularly had infestations of cockroaches and bedbugs onboard. So much for the good old days of car ferrying.

It was in 1953 that Bunny Robertson got the chance to follow his father's lead, by bringing home a new Ludington-based ferry out of a Wisconsin shipyard. Bunny recalled being told by marine superintendent L.H. Kent that he would be appointed master of C&O's new Lake Michigan flagship, the SS *Badger*. Shortly before the ship's sea-trials, Bunny was sent to the Christy yard at Sturgeon Bay, where he spent an exhaustive week becoming acquainted with his new command, examining her from top to bottom. Everything went well during the trials, maiden voyage and all of the civic and corporate ceremonies that followed. Bunny fondly remembered the occasion as being equally exciting for his wife, Florence, and daughter Audrey, as well as for the City of Ludington and its car ferry fleet. A highlight for Robertson was witnessing the signing of the *Badger*'s mortgage and vessel enrollment documents by a large party of attorneys at the federal building in Milwaukee.

In my brief time knowing Captain Robertson, I came to realize that he had enjoyed a challenging 16 years as the *Badger*'s first skipper, and a long, happy retirement. He spent his time working around the house with his wife and helping out his daughter Audrey and her husband, Jim Boals, at their dry cleaning business. Further evidence of Bunny's full life came during my final visit with him. He proudly displayed a recent newspaper clipping with a photo of him posing with a 34-pound king salmon he had caught during an outing with his son-in-law.

On February 13, 1992, I got a telephone call from a good friend, Capt. Gregg Andersen, in Ludington. Immediately upon hearing his tone of voice, my heart sank. I knew the reason for the call. "Hi Art, I've got some bad news for you . . ." he trailed off in a hushed voice. When I was told of Bunny's death, it took my breath away. It was a feeling of great personal loss, yet there was also a selfish element to it. What tore me up inside was that so much more untold history was lost with the passing of Captain Robertson.

After our final interview, we bid each other goodbye on Bunny's front porch. He smiled and shook my hand and said, "Every time you visit you unlock more memories! Last week I had a dream that I was docking the *Badger*. I hadn't tied her up in over 20 years, yet I could see and feel every detail, like I had just left her yesterday!" I knew he was thanking me by the look in his eyes.

As I got into my car he said, "I'll see you next time." Next time never came.

In retrospect, I'm pleased that I recorded all that I could and that I made a difference in an old man's life. My time spent with Bunny has greatly influenced my perspective on the brevity of life and has deepened my appreciation of history more profoundly than he could ever know.

RIDING THE WAVES
A Tribute to the SS Badger

The water's a mirror at first light of day
At the dock she's waiting to get underway
Cast off the lines take a step back in time
Another journey begins

Fiery sunsets and fog shrouded shores
Pulses quicken in gathering storms
Sharp blue horizons starlit black skies
Ship whistles and seagull cries

> *(Chorus)*
> *Riding the waves wherever they take us*
> *Rough seas roll in but they won't break us*
> *Alive with her spirit and all that it makes us*
> *We're riding the waves*

Steady and strong through the wind and the waves
Her decks guard the secrets of thousands of days
Travelers have stories as they come and go
But her crew is truly her soul

Preserved for tomorrow a link to the past
Escaping the rush in a world going too fast
The thrill of the voyage, the joy of return
And always so much to learn

> *(Chorus)*

A living legend, a ship true and tried
She's the people who keep her and serve her with pride
Two distant ports always there at the end
To welcome her home once again

> *(Chorus)*

— Words and music by Kari Karr, December 2007

Kari Karr, former director of marketing for Lake Michigan Carferry, captures the *Badger*'s spirit in a song she wrote honoring the ship's crew. Her lyrics echo the sentiment felt by past and present crew and the passengers that have sailed aboard the *Badger*.

Appendix B

GENERAL SPECIFICATIONS

SS *Badger* and SS *Spartan*

BADGER—US Registry No. 265156
Hull No. 370

SPARTAN—US Registry No. 264500
Hull No. 369

Builder: Christy Corporation, Sturgeon Bay, Wisconsin

Keel Laid: April 19, 1951
Launched: September 6, 1952
Delivered: March 21, 1953

Keel Laid: December 19, 1950
Launched: January 4, 1952
Delivered: October 23, 1952

Length: Overall: 410' 6" Between Perpendiculars: 388'   Registered: 396.7'
Breadth: Overall: 60' 4"   Molded: 59'6"   Registered: 59.7'
Depth: Molded (to main deck): 24'   Registered: 20.3'
Draft: Light: 14'   Loaded (maximum mean): 18' 6"
Tonnage: Gross: 4244   Net: 2033   Displacement: 8860   Total Deadweight: 3560
Railroad Car Capacity (as built): 32 40-foot cars, avg. max. capacity each: 80 tons
Car Deck Overhead Clearance (above rails, as built): 18'

PROPULSION SYSTEM

The ships' propulsion system is comprised of two steeple-compound Skinner Unaflow reciprocating steam engines, built by the Skinner Engine Company of Erie, Pennsylvania.

Four Cylinders—22 1/2" high pressure, 51" low pressure—are arranged in "steeple" formation with both cylinders served by a single cylinder head. The piston stroke is 26 inches. Normal operating horsepower (each engine) is 3500 at 125 revolutions per minute or a continuous overload capacity of 4,000 horsepower at 130 rpm for a total overload capacity of 8,000 horsepower.

Steam is furnished by four D-type two-drum watertube boilers built by the Foster-Wheeler Corporation of Carteret, New Jersey. Each unit has a normal evaporation of 29,500 pounds of steam per hour. Operational steam temperature is 750 degrees Fahrenheit and 450 psig at the superheater outlet, with feed temperature of 225 degrees at the economizer inlet. Exhaust from the engines is to a vacuum of 27 1/2 inches. Each boiler is provided with a Clarage forced-draft fan feeding air at a rate of 20,000 cubic feet per minute. The furnaces are coal-fired by Hoffman Firite spreader-type automatic stokers. The coal bunker has a capacity of 425 tons. Coal-handling equipment is furnished by Stephens Adamson Corporation and consists of two pan-type conveyors discharging into a pair of coal crushers. These in turn discharge the crushed and sized coal through a watertight gate onto two Redler L-type conveyors. From there the coal is discharged through four screw-type conveyors that lead to the "day bunkers" located above the individual stoker systems.

As built, the *Badger* and *Spartan* had a pair of Ferguson 4-bladed cast steel propellers, 13 feet 10 inches in diameter, each weighing 13,800 pounds. Loaded service speed was approximately 18 miles per hour.

Appendix C

Profiles and Deck Plans

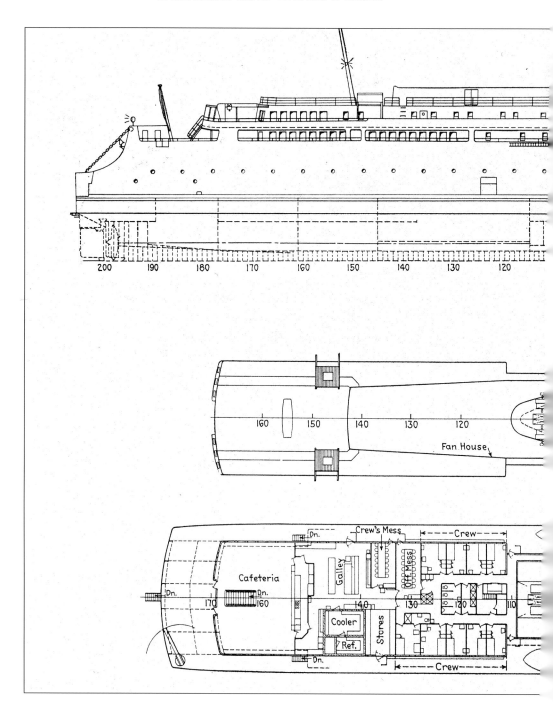

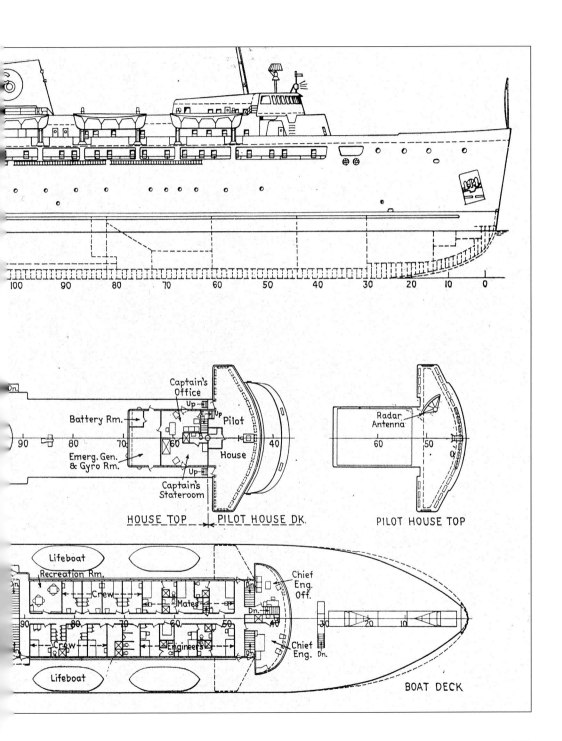

HOUSE TOP | PILOT HOUSE DK.

PILOT HOUSE TOP

BOAT DECK

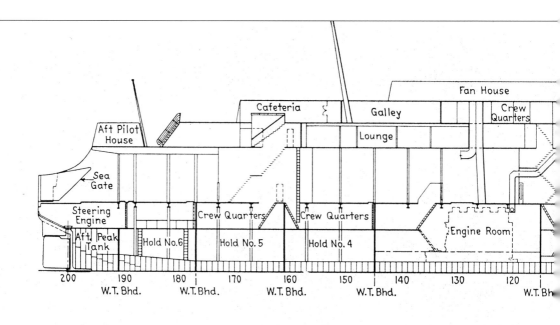

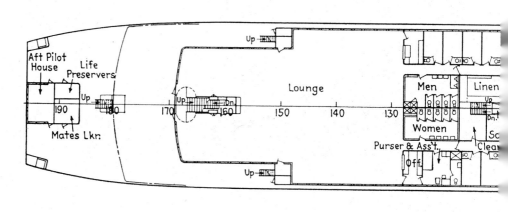

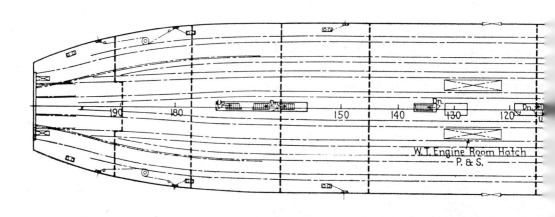

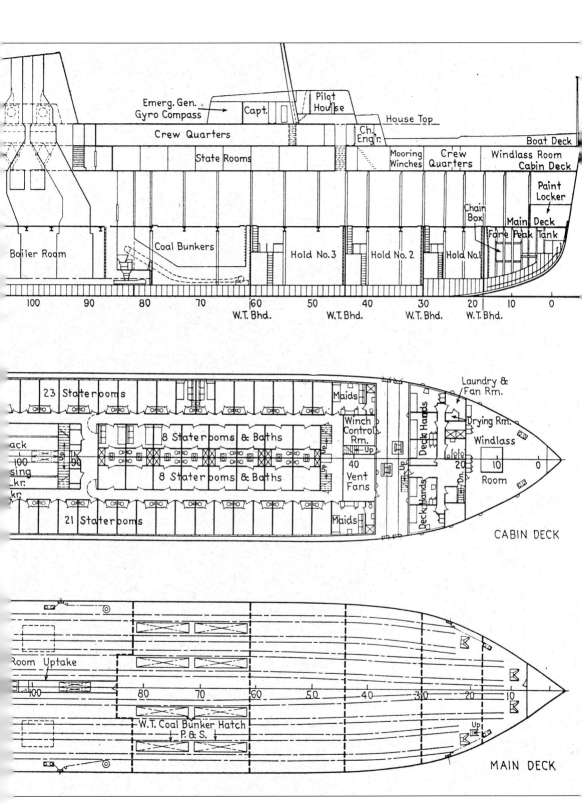

Emerg. Gen.
Gyro Compass
Capt.
Pilot House
House Top
Crew Quarters
Ch. Eng'r.
Boat Deck
State Rooms
Mooring Winches
Crew Quarters
Windlass Room
Cabin Deck
Paint Locker
Chain Box
Main Deck
Fore Peak Tank
Boiler Room
Coal Bunkers
Hold No.3
Hold No. 2
Hold No.1

100   90   80   70   60   50   40   30   20   10   0
W.T. Bhd.   W.T. Bhd.   W.T. Bhd.   W.T. Bhd.

23 Staterooms
Laundry & Fan Rm.
Maids
Drying Rm.
Winch Control Rm.
Windlass
ack
8 Staterooms & Baths
Deck Hands
100
sing
kr.
40 Vent Fans
8 Staterooms & Baths
10 Room
20
Up
Dn.
21 Staterooms
Deckhands
Maids
CABIN DECK

Room Uptake
100   80   70   60   50   40   30   20   10
W.T. Coal Bunker Hatch
P. & S.
Up
MAIN DECK

145

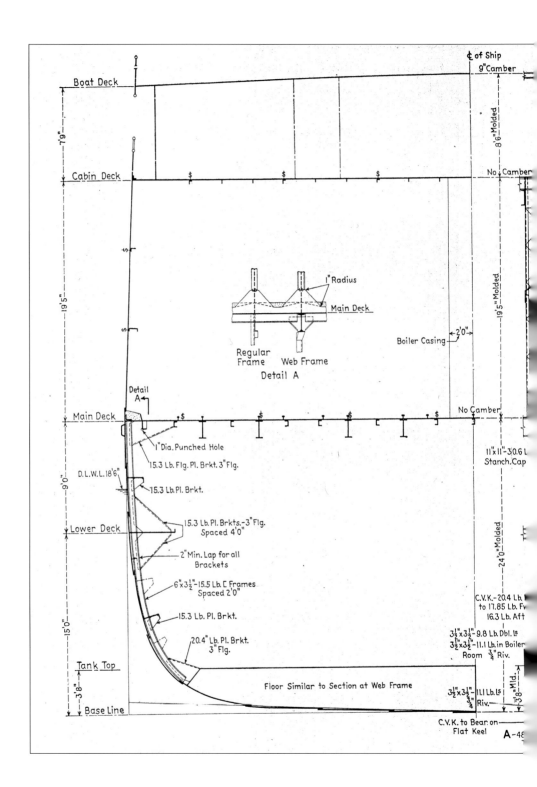

Boat Deck

Cabin Deck

Main Deck

Detail A
A

Lower Deck

Tank Top

Base Line

7'9"

19'5"

9'0"

15'0"

3'8"

₵ of Ship
9" Camber

8'6" Molded

No Camber

1" Radius

Main Deck

Regular   Web Frame
Frame
Detail A

Boiler Casing   2'0"

19'5" Molded

No Camber

1" Dia. Punched Hole

15.3 Lb. Flg. Pl. Brkt. 3" Flg.

15.3 Lb. Pl. Brkt.

D.L.W.L. 18'6"

15.3 Lb. Pl. Brkts.–3" Flg.
Spaced 4'0"

2" Min. Lap for all
Brackets

6"x3½"–15.5 Lb. ⌐ Frames
Spaced 2'0"

15.3 Lb. Pl. Brkt.

20.4 Lb. Pl. Brkt.
3" Flg.

Floor Similar to Section at Web Frame

11"x11"–30.6 L
Stanch. Cap

24'0" Molded

C.V.K.–20.4 Lb.
to 17.85 Lb. Fw
16.3 Lb. Aft

3½"x3½"–9.8 Lb. Dbl. ⌐s
3½"x3½"–11.1 Lb. in Boiler
Room ¾" Riv.

3½"x3½"–11.1 Lb. ⌐s
¾" Riv.

3'8" Mld.

C.V.K. to Bear on
Flat Keel   A-48

146

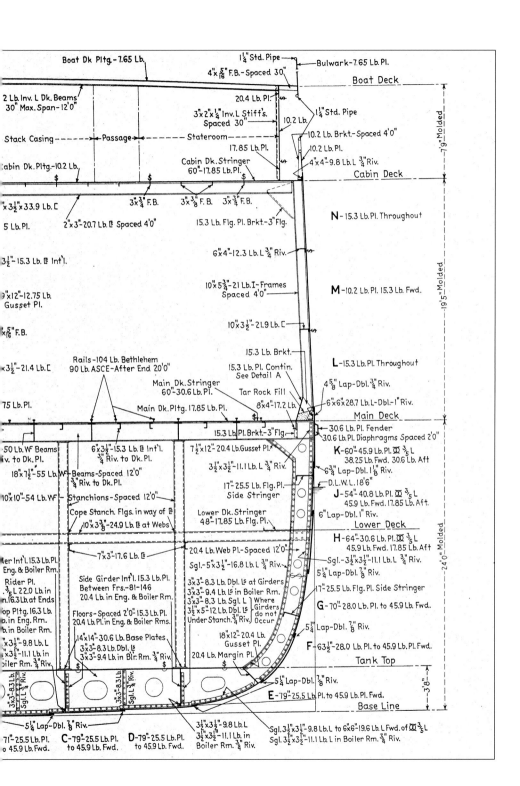

Boat Dk Pltg - 7.65 Lb.

1¼" Std. Pipe

Bulwark - 7.65 Lb. Pl.

4"×⁵⁄₁₆" F.B. - Spaced 30"

Boat Deck

2 Lb. Inv. L Dk. Beams
30" Max. Span - 12'0"

20.4 Lb. Pl.

3"×2"×¼" Inv. L Stiff's.
Spaced 30"

10.2 Lb.

1¼" Std. Pipe

Stack Casing — Passage — Stateroom

10.2 Lb. Brkt. - Spaced 4'0"

10.2 Lb. Pl.

17.85 Lb. Pl.

4"×4"-9.8 Lb. L ¾" Riv.

Cabin Dk. Pltg. - 10.2 Lb.

Cabin Dk. Stringer
60"-17.85 Lb. Pl.

Cabin Deck

×3½"×33.9 Lb. C

3"×¾" F.B.   3"×⅜" F.B.   3"×¾" F.B.

N - 15.3 Lb. Pl. Throughout

5 Lb. Pl.

2"×3"-20.7 Lb. ₢ Spaced 4'0"

15.3 Lb. Flg. Pl. Brkt. - 3" Flg.

3½"-15.3 Lb. ₢ Int'l.

6"×4"-12.3 Lb. L ¾" Riv.

M - 10.2 Lb. Pl. 15.3 Lb. Fwd.

9"×12"-12.75 Lb.
Gusset Pl.

10"×5¾"-21 Lb. I-Frames
Spaced 4'0"

×⁵⁄₁₆" F.B.

10"×3½"-21.9 Lb. C

3½"-21.4 Lb. C

Rails - 104 Lb. Bethlehem
90 Lb. ASCE - After End 20'0"

15.3 Lb. Brkt.

L - 15.3 Lb. Pl. Throughout

15.3 Lb. Pl. Contin.
See Detail A

4⅝" Lap-Dbl. ¾" Riv.

Main Dk. Stringer
60"-30.6 Lb. Pl.

Tar Rock Fill

6"×6"-28.7 Lb. L-Dbl.-1" Riv.

75 Lb. Pl.

Main Dk. Pltg. 17.85 Lb. Pl.

8"×4"-17.2 Lb.

Main Deck

15.3 Lb. Pl. Brkt. - 3" Flg.

30.6 Lb. Pl. Fender
30.6 Lb. Pl. Diaphragms Spaced 2'0"

50 Lb. WF Beams
iv. to Dk. Pl.

6"×3½"-15.3 Lb. ₢ Int'l.
¾" Riv. to Dk. Pl.

7½"×12"-20.4 Lb. Gusset Pl.

K - 60"-45.9 Lb. Pl. ⊠ ⅗ L
38.25 Lb. Fwd. 30.6 Lb. Aft

18"×7½"-55 Lb. WF Beams-Spaced 12'0"
¾" Riv. to Dk. Pl.

3½"×3½"-11.1 Lb. L ¾" Riv.

6¾" Lap-Dbl. 1⅛" Riv.

17"-25.5 Lb. Flg. Pl.
Side Stringer

D.L.W.L. 18'6"

10"×10"-54 Lb. WF Stanchions - Spaced 12'0"

J - 54"-40.8 Lb. Pl. ⊠ ⅗ L
45.9 Lb. Fwd. 17.85 Lb. Aft.

Cope Stanch. Flgs. in way of ₢
10"×3⅜"-24.9 Lb. ₢ at Webs

Lower Dk. Stringer
48"-17.85 Lb. Flg. Pl.

6" Lap-Dbl. 1" Riv.

Lower Deck

H - 64"-30.6 Lb. Pl. ⊠ ⅗ L
45.9 Lb. Fwd. 17.85 Lb. Aft

er Int'l. 15.3 Lb. Rm.
Eng. & Boiler Rm.

7"×3"-17.6 Lb. ₢

20.4 Lb. Web Pl. - Spaced 12'0"

Sgl. - 3½"×3½"-11.1 Lb. L ¾" Riv.

Rider Pl.
₢ L 22.0 Lb. in
.16.3 Lb. at Ends

Side Girder Int'l. 15.3 Lb. Pl.
Between Frs.-81-146
20.4 Lb. in Eng. & Boiler Rm.

Sgl.-5"×3½"-16.8 Lb. L ¾" Riv.

5¼" Lap-Dbl. ⅞" Riv.

op Pltg. 16.3 Lb.
.in Eng. Rm.
b. in Boiler Rm.

Floors-Spaced 2'0"-15.3 Lb. Pl.
20.4 Lb. Pl. in Eng. & Boiler Rms.

3"×3"-8.3 Lb. Dbl. ₢s at Girders
3"×3"-9.4 Lb. ₢s in Boiler Rm.
3"×3"-8.3 Lb. Sgl. ₢
3½"×5"-12 Lb. Dbl. ₢s
Under Stanch. ¾" Riv.

Where
Girders
do not
Occur

17"-25.5 Lb. Flg. Pl. Side Stringer

G - 70"-28.0 Lb. Pl. to 45.9 Lb. Fwd.

×3½"-9.8 Lb. in
×3½"-11.1 Lb in
oiler Rm. ¾" Riv.

14"×14"-30.6 Lb. Base Plates
3"×3"-8.3 Lb. Dbl. ₢s
3"×3"-9.4 Lb. in Blr. Rm. ¾" Riv.

18"×12"-20.4 Lb.
Gusset Pl.

5¼" Lap-Dbl. ⅞" Riv.

20.4 Lb. Margin Pl.

F - 63½"-28.0 Lb. Pl. to 45.9 Lb. Pl. Fwd.

Tank Top

3"×3"-8.3 Lb.
Sgl. L ¾" Riv.

3"×3"-8.3 Lb.
Sgl. L ¾" Riv.

5¼" Lap-Dbl. ⅞" Riv.

E - 79"-25.5 Lb. Pl. to 45.9 Lb. Pl. Fwd.

Base Line

5¼" Lap-Dbl. ⅞" Riv.

71"-25.5 Lb. Pl.
o 45.9 Lb. Fwd.

C - 79"-25.5 Lb. Pl.
to 45.9 Lb. Fwd.

D - 79"-25.5 Lb. Pl.
to 45.9 Lb. Fwd.

3½"×3½"-9.8 Lb. L
3½"×3½"-11.1 Lb. in
Boiler Rm. ¾" Riv.

Sgl. 3½"×3½"-9.8 Lb. L to 6"×6"-19.6 Lb. L Fwd. of ⊠ ⅗ L
Sgl. 3½"×3½"-11.1 Lb. L in Boiler Rm. ¾" Riv.

7'-9" Molded

19'-5" Molded

24'-0" Molded

3'-8"

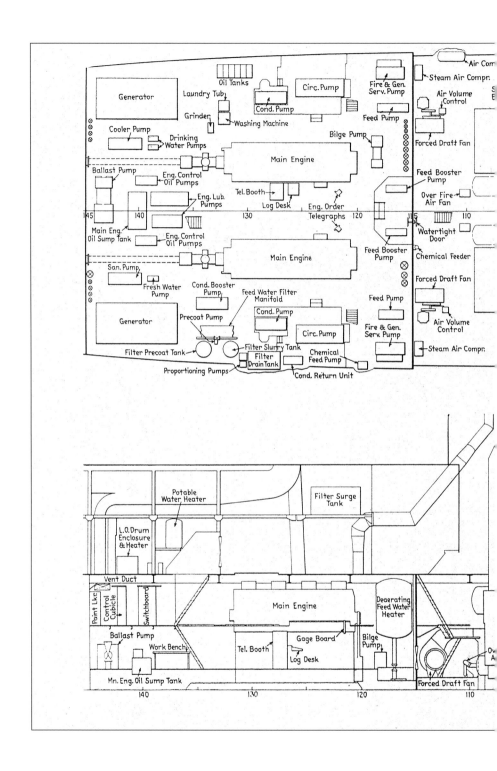

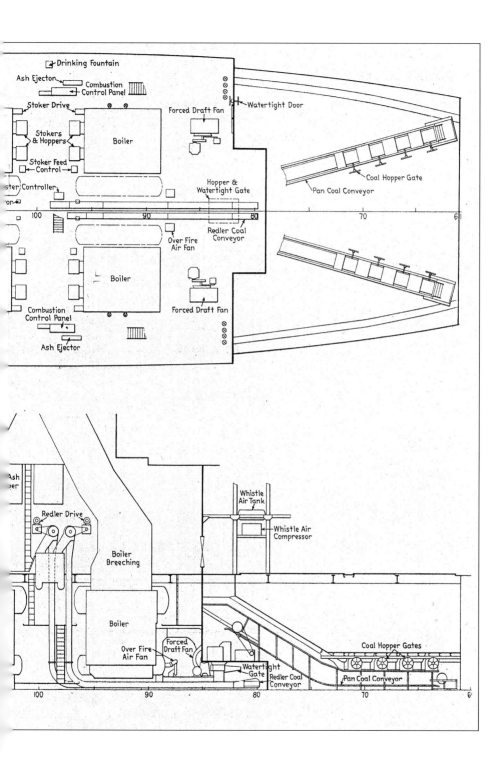

149

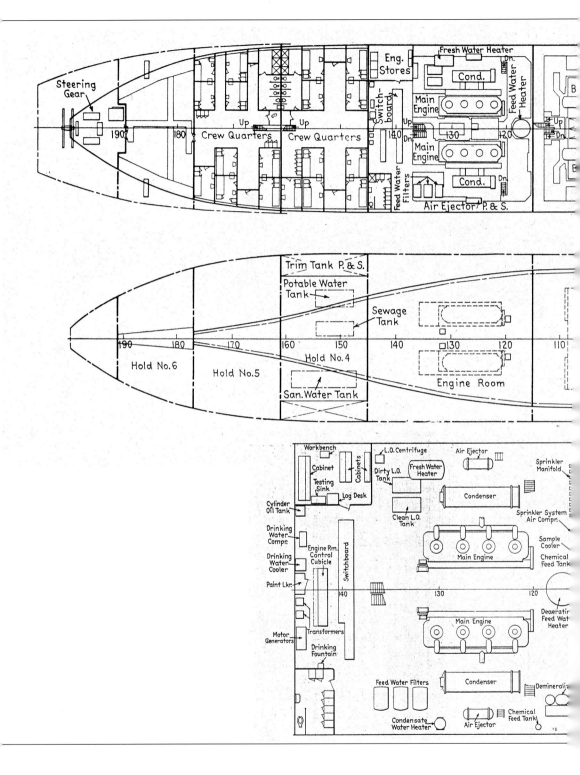

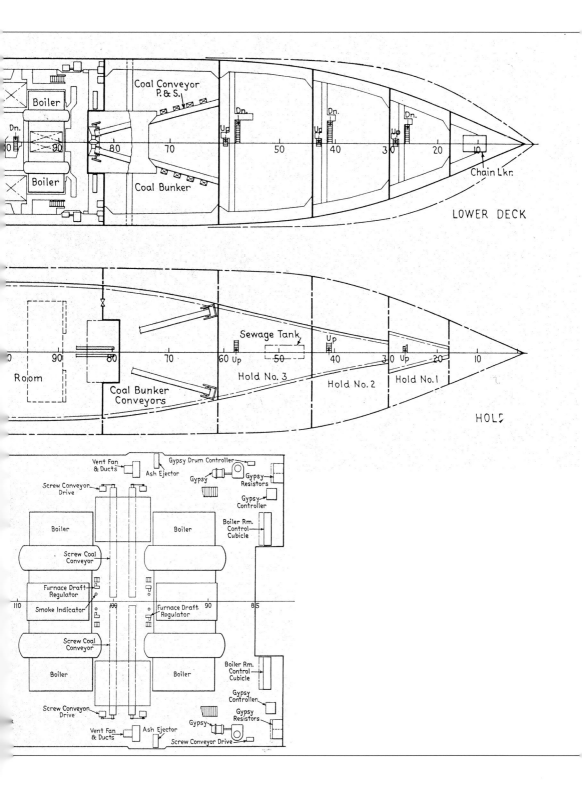

LOWER DECK

HOL·

151

DESIGN FEATURES OF THE SKINNER COMPOUND UNAFLOW MARINE STEAM ENGINE

1. Inspection cover.

2. Positive piston rod lock.

3. Four inspection ports for piston rings.

4. High-pressure piston, alloy iron.

5. High-pressure cylinder liner, forged steel, chromium plated. Taper bored to compensate for expansion due to temperature gradient. Cooled by low-pressure steam.

6. High-pressure cylinder casing, alloy iron.

7. High-pressure piston rod steam packing with special bronze rings. Cooled by low-pressure steam.

8. Piston rod, forged alloy steel, ground to fine finish.

9. Steam-tight transfer valve, transfers steam to low-pressure cylinder after expansion in high-pressure cylinder.
Steam valve (not shown) admits steam to high-pressure cylinder from manifold.
Auxiliary exhaust valve (not shown), relieves compression in low-pressure cylinder when reversing, and may be held open to permit removal of water from self-draining high-pressure cylinder and head.
All valves are steam-tight, double-seat, telescopic poppet type, with free seat. Permanently tight, regardless of variation in pressure and temperature.

10. Valve cage, steel, with integral seats. All valves mounted in cages for convenience in handling.

11. Return motion mechanism, hydraulic controls, for lead and cut-off.

12. Dual camshafts for accurate timing and positive control of lead and cut-off. All cams, rollers and gears are hardened and ground to close tolerances. Rollers have line contact on cams. Pressure lubrication of all cam mechanism.

13. Control lever, cut-off ahead (or lead astern). Control shifts camshafts hydraulically for minimum effort and quick response.

14. Control lever, cut-off astern (or lead ahead).

15. Throttle valve control lever (hydraulic control).

16. Bored crosshead guide, concentrically rabbeted to low-pressure cylinder for permanent alignment.

17. Crosshead shoe, babbitted top and bottom. This construction allows continuous full-load operation either ahead or astern.

18. Crosshead and pins, single-piece high-carbon steel forging.

19. Permanent indicator reducing motion, with detent, for each cylinder. Permits taking indicator cards at any time without stopping the engine.

20. Connecting rod, forged steel, forked at upper end to reduce height, with heat-treated fitted bolts.

21. Frame weldment, box type, provides rigidity and total enclosure for cleanliness.

22. Base weldment, heavy construction for rigidity.

23. Dry sump to prevent oil loss and oxidation due to splash.

24. Injectors for steam cylinder oil. Two for each high-pressure cylinder.

25. Permanent double ground joints, head to high-pressure and low-pressure cylinders. No gaskets.

26. Steam piping, designed to permit expansion.

27. Cylinder head, steam-jacketed, cast steel.

28. Throttle valve, balanced for ease of operation.

29. Exhaust manifold, fabricated steel.

30. Low-pressure piston, fabricated steel. Fitted with sectional piston rings and followers with wear-band inserts. Rings and followers removable through bulkhead opening.

31. Drain for condensate under low-pressure piston.

32. Exhaust ports, ample area to manifold.

33. Low-pressure cylinder, alloy iron, taper bored to compensate for expansion due to temperature gradient.

34. Bulkhead, split for removal through crankcase to provide access to low-pressure piston and cylinder.

35. Bulkhead and vacuum packing, split cases to facilitate removal.

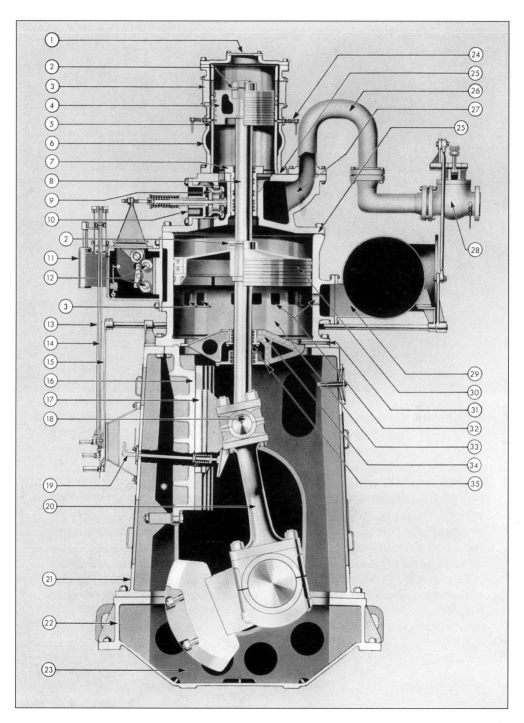

One of the two 4,000-horsepower Skinner Compound Unaflow Marine Steam Engines installed on the *Spartan*, designed for steam conditions of 440 psig, 740 degrees F.T.T., at the throttle, exhausting to 27.5 inches vacuum.

Chesapeake & Ohio Railway Company's car ferries *Badger* and *Spartan* are the largest on the Great Lakes. Each vessel is propelled by Skinner Compound Unaflow Marine Steam Engines developing a total normal of 8,000 horsepower.

HIGH AND LOW PRESSURE DIAGRAMS

HIGH-PRESSURE DIAGRAM

A — Steam valve opens
A to B — Admission to high-pressure cylinder
B — Steam valve closes (high-pressure cut-off)
B to C — Expansion in high-pressure cylinder
C — Transfer valve opens (high-pressure exhaust)
C to D — Exhaust from high-pressure cylinder to low-pressure cylinder
D — Transfer valve closes
D to A — Compression in high-pressure cylinder

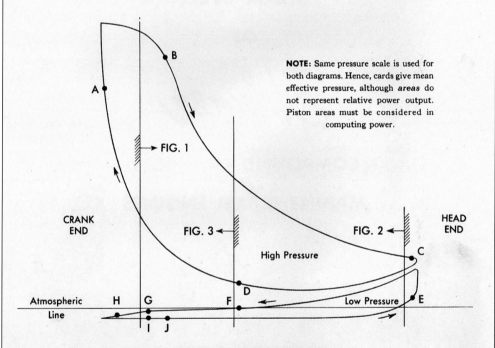

NOTE: Same pressure scale is used for both diagrams. Hence, cards give mean effective pressure, although *areas* do not represent relative power output. Piston areas must be considered in computing power.

LOW-PRESSURE DIAGRAM

E — Transfer valve opens (low-pressure admission)
E to F — Admission to low-pressure cylinder
F — Transfer valve closes (low-pressure cut-off)
F to G — Expansion in low-pressure cylinder
G — Exhaust ports uncovered in low-pressure cylinder
G to I — Exhaust from low-pressure cylinder to condenser
H — Auxiliary exhaust valve opens
H to J — Auxiliary exhaust from low-pressure cylinder to condenser
J — Auxiliary exhaust valve closes
J to E — Compression in low-pressure cylinder

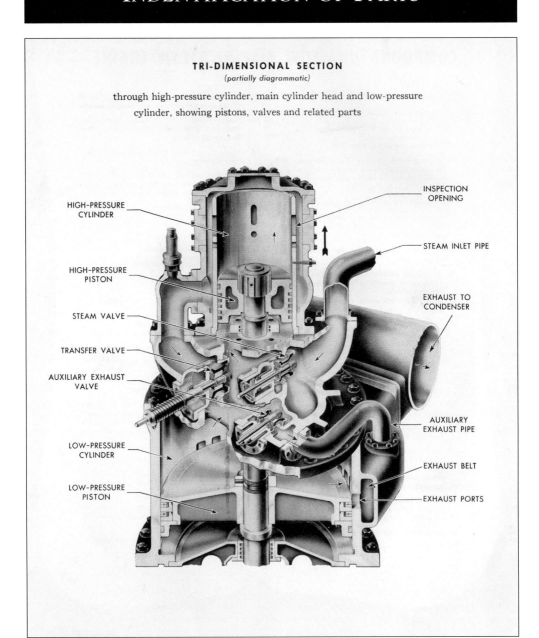

TRI-DIMENSIONAL SECTION
(partially diagrammatic)

through high-pressure cylinder, main cylinder head and low-pressure
cylinder, showing pistons, valves and related parts

HIGH-PRESSURE CYLINDER

HIGH-PRESSURE PISTON

STEAM VALVE

TRANSFER VALVE

AUXILIARY EXHAUST VALVE

LOW-PRESSURE CYLINDER

LOW-PRESSURE PISTON

INSPECTION OPENING

STEAM INLET PIPE

EXHAUST TO CONDENSER

AUXILIARY EXHAUST PIPE

EXHAUST BELT

EXHAUST PORTS

STEAM VALVE OPEN
AUXILIARY EXHAUST VALVE OPEN

Steam valve open
Auxiliary exhaust valve open
Transfer valve closed
Power stroke upward

High-pressure steam acting on bottom of high-pressure piston.
Low-pressure steam exhausting to condenser through exhaust ports
and auxiliary exhaust valve.

Transfer valve open
Steam valve closed
Auxiliary exhaust valve closed
Power stroke downward

Steam exhausting from high-pressure cylinder into low-pressure cylinder for further expansion.

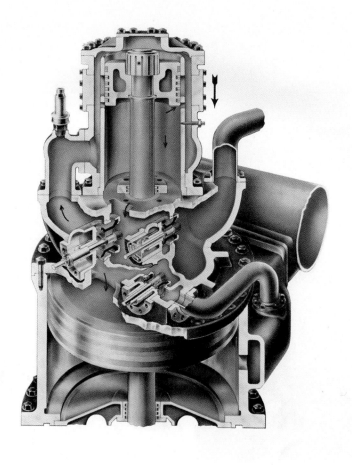

All valves closed
Power stroke downward

Steam continuing to expand in low-pressure cylinder.
Compression beginning in high-pressure cylinder.

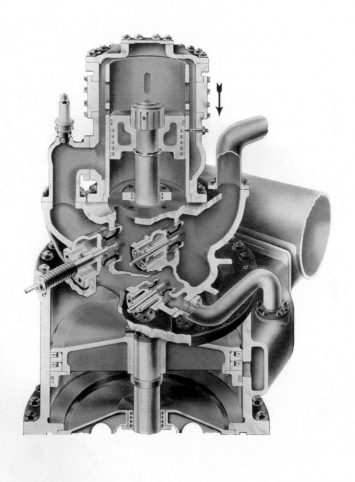

Suggested Reading

BOOKS

Christianson, Carl Raymond. *My First Seventy-Two Years*. Sturgeon Bay, WI: the author, 1975.
Elve, Steven Dale. *Bridging the Waves*. Lowell, MI: the author, 1989.
Frederickson, Arthur C. and Lucy F. *Pictorial History of the C&O Train and Auto Ferries and Pere Marquette Line Steamers*. Frankfort, MI, revised edition, 1965.
Hilton, George W. *The Great Lakes Car Ferries*. Berkeley, CA: Howell-North, 1962; Montevallo Historical Press, 2003.
Ludington Daily News. *Ludington's Carferries-The Rise, Decline & Rebirth of a Great Lakes Fleet*. Marceline, MO: Walsworth Publishing, 1997.
Mailer, Stan. *Green Bay & Western*. Edmonds, WA: Hundman Publishing, 1989.
Zimmermann, Karl. *Lake Michigan's Railroad Car Ferries*. Andover, NJ: Andover Junction Publications, 1993.

PERIODICALS

Vande Vusse, Robert. The Centennial of the Pere Marquette 15 (entire issue), *Rails*, Number 2, 1996, Pere Marquette Historical Society.

HISTORICAL ORGANIZATIONS AND WEBSITES

Carferries of the Great Lakes, www.carferries.com.
Chesapeake and Ohio Historical Society, www.cohs.org.
Door County Maritime Museum, www.dcmm.org.
Pere Marquette Historical Society, www.pmhistsoc.org.
Port of Ludington Maritime Museum, www.ludingtonmaritimemuseum.org.
Wisconsin Marine Historical Society, wmhs.org.
Wisconsin Maritime Museum at Manitowoc, www.wisconsinmaritime.org.

REFERENCES

Bulletins and Periodicals

Launch Program, SS *Badger*. Christy Corporation, Cleveland, OH, Chesapeake & Ohio Railway Co., 1952.
Marine Engineering, New York, NY, Simmons-Boardman, March 1953.
Skinner Compound Unaflow Marine Steam Engines, Erie, PA, Skinner Engine Co., 1953.

Newspapers

Door County Advocate, July 6, 1950, Sept 21, 1950, October 12, 1950, November 16, 1950, November 24, 1950, December 19, 1950, August 28, 1952, September 4, 1952, September 9, 1952.
Green Bay Press-Gazette, September 6, 1952.
Ludington Daily News, March 12, 1953.
Manitowoc Herald-Times, July 1, 1952, March 21, 1953, March 23, 1953.
Milwaukee Journal, March 17, 1953, March 25, 1953.

Interviews

Oral History interview with Capt. Bernard A. Robertson, May 4, 1991, at Ludington, MI.
Oral History Interview with Capt. Ernest G. Barth, November 10, 1989; February 17, 2001, at Ludington, MI.
Interview with C. Ray Christianson, July 22, 1983, at Sturgeon Bay, WI.